THE ATLANTIC CRITICAL REVIEW

QUARTERLY

A Peer Reviewed Journal Indexed in
MLA Directory of Periodicals

APRIL – JUNE 2014

VOLUME 13 NUMBER 2

ATLANTIC

PUBLISHERS & DISTRIBUTORS (P) LTD

CONTRIBUTORS

Alan Johnson, Department of English & Philosophy, Idaho State University, 921 S. 8th Ave./Pocatello, ID 83209-8056 (USA) Idaho.

Rama Kundu, UGC Emeritus Fellow, Professor of English [retired], Burdwan University, Burdwan-713104, West Bengal.

Aditi Bhardwaj, Assistant Professor (Department of English), The IIS University, Gurukul Marg, SFS, Mansarovar, Jaipur-302020; [R] W/o Mr. Pradhuman Singh, Plot no. 15, Flat No. 3, Satyam Enclave, Saanwra Vihar, Near H-Block Siddharth Nagar, Jaipur, Rajasthan.

Mani Meitei, Professor & Head, Department of English, Manipur University, Imphal-795003, Manipur.

Arindam Modak, Assistant Professor of English, Department of Humanities and Social Sciences, National Institute of Technology, Durgapur-713209; [R] National Institute of Technology Durgapur, Quarters No. DS-6, C, Durgapur-713209, West Bengal.

Sunita Sinha, Associate Professor, Department of English, Women's College, Samastipur, Bihar. [R] 402, Rameswaran Apartments, Miss Mandal Compound, East Boring Canal Road, Patna-800001, Bihar.

Debesh Thakur, Teacher in English. Poet & Playwright in Bengali, Chaplin Scholar, 47, Kalibazar, Burdwan, West Bengal-713101.

THE ATLANTIC CRITICAL REVIEW
VOLUME 13 NUMBER 2 (APRIL-JUNE 2014)

CONTENTS

Local Writing is World Writing: Reflections on Literary Studies in a Global Age

ALAN JOHNSON

Globalization is "a set of social processes" that lead to "the expansion and intensification of social relations and consciousness across world-time and world-space."

–Manfred Steger

The Local and the Global

IN my years of teaching, I've come across an interesting dichotomy when it comes to interpreting literary works. Some readers will respond to a text they've never heard of by saying, "That really opened up my eyes! I didn't know anything about this place, or even that there were people writing about it." Other readers of the same text will complain, "Why do we have to read *this* novel (or poem)? Why don't we read books about *our* lives?" Both views are, I think, legitimate, and have more to do with today's diverse readership than with the works themselves. In my experience, the former view prevails, thankfully, though there are understandable reasons for the latter. We all agree, for example, with Virginia Woolf's observation in the 1920s that women were excluded from forming and appreciating a tradition of women's literature, so that to say "Why must I read yet another male author's book and not one by a woman, about the lives of women," is a crucial insight in the history of writing and reading. There are, in other words, political, cultural and economic reasons for why a society values certain literary texts over others, even when these "others" merit equal (or more) attention.

But I am still not always clear about how to respond to readers whose main complaint about a well-known literary work is that it does not speak to them, when their own peers declare the opposite. Although this has something to do with each reader's own subjective outlook, we can't separate the text from the act of reading: they are intimately connected.

A case in point is Mark Twain's *Huckleberry Finn,* the first American novel (1876) to use a distinctly American vernacular. Instructors often have their students compare the nineteenth-century audience response to the novel to today's readership, which leads us inevitably into matters of race, but also of gender and sexuality. Whereas the debate in Twain's day was about the "literary value" of the novel, today's debate is over matters that did not seem so obvious to a white, male-dominated readership at the time. Twain scholar Shelley Fisher Fishkin has called the novel an early example of linguistic hybridity, with Huck intuitively responding to, and using, African American idioms to produce a distinctly American rhythm and outlook.

I won't pretend to propose a resolution to this debate here. I offer these points only in order to provoke our thoughts concerning our own personal as well as cultural biases. My main point should be a familiar one, namely that re-interpretation never ends, depending as it does on different times and places and individuals. *Hamlet*, as we know, has fallen in and out of favour as Shakespeare's greatest play, depending on where and when it was produced and interpreted, and according to what other texts and values surrounded it. Readers, in other words, have always read comparatively. Above all, our efforts as readers and instructors, as parties to the human predicament, must be to avoid narrow-minded views.

Another related debate concerns the apparent paradox that a writer's description of a very localized, idiosyncratic community often finds enthusiastic readers around the world, in cultures that cannot grasp all of the implications of that place's idiosyncrasies. Why should a very regional characterization of southern Mississippi by William Faulkner prove to be so influential? Why would a young Gabriel Garcia Marquez read Faulkner and be inspired to paint his own influential portrait of Colombia? The apparent paradox is a familiar one, much like the advice to "write what you know" and "write the local". We know that the real truth to emerge from a literary work derives from its credibility and humanity, not its grasp of politics or of the world. This is what we believe, and this is what we teach our students.

But the matter is not so simple. This apparent paradox continues to generate discussion especially in relation to the politics of narration. If literature is indeed meant to be true to a global "spirit of being human", why should it then be caught up in the politics of nation, or class, or race, or religion? Why is Joyce Cary's novel *Mr. Johnson*, praised by Western critics when it appeared in 1939, no longer taught? Why is Conrad's *Heart of Darkness*, which is still widely taught, so controversial? Chinua Achebe famously decries both the novels for their characteristically European indictment of African cultures. The American critic Gerald Graff writes candidly about how his views about *Heart of Darkness* changed after reading Achebe's and others' criticism of the book. Instead of jettisoning the novel from his courses, however, Graff chose to teach it alongside Achebe's great 1958 novel *Things Fall Apart* to activate his students' evaluative skills and to "teach the conflicts". Achebe's novel paints a far different picture of Africa than what he calls Conrad's "racist" images. Nonetheless, as Graff observes, the ghost of Conrad's novel is hard to miss in reading Achebe's.

Such considerations compel us to ask, if some texts, like Cary's, are happily dropped from the canon, are there others that are unfairly treated? In the U.S., this frequently occurs at the level of local township libraries, which are funded by the community. Parents frequently call for the banning of a young adult novel on the grounds that it offends their particular sensibility or culture, and the library sometimes complies, which then generates a big debate. In American universities there is no forced banning, but rather self-imposed restrictions, such as when professors, often with good reason, decide that a text is chauvinistic or offensive in some particular way. In India, we all know that such cases are politicized, as with the Shiv Sena's ban on a biography of Shivaji by an American historian, or the group's recent agitation to similarly remove a novel by Rohinton Mistry from Bombay University's curriculum.

We could go on with such examples, but to return to my point: The debate over what to teach is related to the supposed paradox I mentioned, of the local-global nexus, of Faulkner being read in Spanish or French, just as Flaubert is popularly read in English, despite the common reader's relative ignorance about the book's social-historical context. I say this is an "apparent" paradox to make clear that in my view this is not, in fact, a paradox, but instead a confusion that results from our asking the wrong kinds of questions. The question of canonicity is not a zero-sum game. Rather than simply say that *Madame Bovary* is "obviously" a great work, we need to ask how this greatness has been conferred—not so much to question that valuation as to dissect it so that we don't fall into the trap of false dichotomies. This leads us, of course, to the problem of aesthetics and artistic taste, which has long been pondered by the likes of Horace and Abhinavagupta, Hume and Adorno, a topic much beyond the scope of this essay. Instead, I want to focus on the fact that we should all ask ourselves why we are reading the texts we read. Part of this has to do with money, namely the costs and rewards of publication. Perhaps more important, in my view, is the fact that texts are never read in isolation, but rather speak to other texts—the ones the text explicitly or implicitly invokes as well as the ones that an individual reader has read and thus brings to the conversation. We may not find explicit references to Lawrence Sterne's *Tristram Shandy* or to Gunther Grass's *The Tin Drum* in Rushdie's *Midnight's Children*, for example, but we can't miss their presence in the novel. Reading and interpretation have always been acts of comparison. It's unavoidable, and to believe that a text, even scripture, has no other textual comparisons is a dangerous belief. This is the dark side of localism, when texts are believed by politically minded, bullying people to require no evaluation, that they simply *are*. Full stop, end of debate. The development of comparative literature as a discipline was, in part, a response to this kind of regionalism that encourages intolerance, as happened in Europe leading up to the Second World War, and as continues to happen, with varying intensity, in every part of the world.

David Damrosch observes that we really have three canons when we teach literature, the "hypercanon, countercanon, and shadow canon" (45). The hypercanon is his term for the old mainstays of Western literature in English—Chaucer and Shakespeare, Melville and Joyce and Woolf, as well as more recent arrivals like J.M. Coetzee and Nadine Gordimer. Far from being superseded by new authors, these big names are, as Damrosch points out, revisited again and again, albeit in fresh ways. Then there's the countercanon, made up of formerly neglected and often new voices, such as bestselling writers Achebe, Garcia Marquez, Rushdie and Arundhati Roy, as well as comparatively lesser-known but increasingly recognized writers like Tsitsi Dangarembga, Clarice Lispector, and Shashi Deshpande. (Some of the latter—Rushdie, Achebe, Garcia Marquez—have, in fact, achieved the near-status of the hypercanonical.) Finally, Damrosch identifies a shadow canon that is composed of once-familiar but currently sidelined Western writers studied by an older generation of scholars, writers like William Hazlitt and Robert Southey.

While the countercanon reflects the success of re-interpretations that have arisen in the wake of literary theory, from the 1960s to the present, and also reflects geopolitical changes, Damrosch points out that we reproduce some of the same problems we wanted to avoid. Thus, a single author comes to stand in for an entire nation, and some of these authors attain the same star status as the Western writers they've displaced. This reflects the practical problems of available publications, the time we have available to read, study and teach, and the need to attract students to classes that offer texts they've never heard of. But even within these limits, we should, Damrosch rightly says, do our best to expand our own and our students' reading horizons. He cites the example of offering (in a typical U.S. university) a class on Joyce, but in a comparativist context—Ibsen and Proust, surely, but also Japanese author Higuchi Ichiyo and India's own Tagore.

To teach comparatively raises another challenge, at least for most teachers and students, and that is translation. To what degree can we base our interpretations on the translation of a given text? One can't possibly read all great literature in the original. But the quality of translations varies, and texts themselves are shaped by the translator. Rather than lament this condition, we should embrace it, argues Damrosch. But we should also, as Haun Saussy points out, reveal the extent to which every text is, in a sense, a translation—not only of life's experiences, but of the text's intertextual influences. If I am an American writer who loves and is subtly influenced by Ibsen, I'll need to rely on a good translation from the Swedish. Then, too, there is the "translation" from page to stage. A few years ago I saw an excellent performance of Ibsen's *Hedda Gabler* at the Prithvi Theatre in Mumbai. It was as good a production as one can find, yet it's no doubt different from one in New York or, indeed, Copenhagen. Directorial inflections, tonal inflections, set design—all contribute to shape a unique but still universal production of the play. Novels, too, are translated as we read: How is one to interpret a work in English that is "Kafkaesque," for example? Kafka wrote in German about his Hungarian-Jewish experience set in early twentieth-century Prague. How can that relate to a novel published in the U.S. in English decades later? If a writer uses phrases from a foreign language in the original, as is common, how are we to treat that? Kafka's multicultural experience is, it seems to me, eminently suited to precisely the aim of appreciating the global dimension of literature. We are, to use Rushdie's insight, really all "translated" people, with an often unacknowledged weight of centuries of influence by cultures far beyond the shores we happen to inhabit. After all, Kalidasa, Sophocles, and Virgil have shaped countless writers around the globe. Martin Luther King, Jr., learned to admire his nineteenth-century compatriot Henry David Thoreau's staunch civil disobedience by reading Gandhi. And so on.

Literature has, then, always been globalized, and I believe we need to acknowledge this without losing sight of a writer's local environment. That, of course, is easier said than done. If, for example, I want to understand a Dalit Gujarati poet as deeply as possible, and even if I read this poet in translation, I will still need to learn something about his or her cultural community and personal circumstances. At the same time, I will want to appreciate the poet's links to voices far beyond his or her locale. I believe that today, with the advent of heightened forms of globalization and its attendant technological tools, we are in a unique place in terms of literary studies. Translations are picking up, influences are ever more global, and readers enjoy reading about experiences and cultures very different from their own. Perhaps the single biggest effect of today's version of globalization is on language, with the advent of Hinglish, Spanglish, and other creoles.

But the process of globalization is a multi-limbed hydra, contentious and hard to define. On a Fulbright stay in India, I had hoped to determine the extent to which literature, and departments of literature, have been shaped by this development by comparing changes in the cultural, curricular, and pedagogical experiences of India and America. Some developments are obvious. A few years ago, hardly any American college student knew about Bollywood or Chinese art or Turkish literature or *bhangra*. In my classrooms today, even in a regional, rural-based institution in the western state of Idaho, I find that students have heard of these and are interested in them. For someone like me who enjoys Bollywood film and its music, it is especially refreshing to find many American students who share this enjoyment.

This may seem to be a superficial change. Today, it seems that all urban students, whether in Mumbai or New York, have mobile phones stuck to their ears, wear jeans, and write in text messages. Is this really a sea change, or just another fashion? On the other hand, there's no denying the radical economic restructuring of the planet, and cultural change, as we know, is often part of this. There is clearly something different about our world today than existed just a decade ago, and that is that we are resembling each other more and more. We can debate the merits of this development, but not that it has occurred. Culturally, film and music reflect the most obvious changes, with Bollywood and Hollywood influencing one another, and with multi-lingual, multi-cultural stars like Shakira finding fans around the planet. Rapper Snoop Dogg appears in a Hindi film, A.R. Rahman wins an Oscar for a British director's interpretation of an Indian novelist's fable about modern India, and Shah Rukh Khan saves victims of Hurricane Katrina. At the same time, multinational corporations such as America's Monsanto, with assets larger than those of most countries, are relentless in their efforts to resist environmental, trade, and labour restrictions in order to fill their shareholders' pockets.

Perhaps most importantly for our literary interest is the fact that globalization, as Susie O'Brien and Imre Szeman have observed, can be grasped only through narrative forms. They also note that the nation, ironically, remains the frame of reference for discussions of globalization despite predictions to the contrary. O'Brien and Szeman therefore challenge us to think beyond the geographically-oriented "imagined community". They claim that the field of post-colonial studies has provided us with perhaps the most useful vocabulary with which to investigate such questions. Yet they warn that to see this development as centered in any particular place (such as the U.S.), as some scholars have claimed, is wrong, for this logic again falls back on the framework of the nation, which does not help us get to real questions concerning the complexities of globality. They note that Michel Foucault's notion of the diffusion of power has been useful in this regard, moving us from a center-periphery paradigm.

To what degree can we agree with O'Brien and Szeman? It is true that "all literature is now global, all literature is a literature of globalization"? One could counter that images are now commonly believed to have displaced words, making our concern with literature an anachronism. Corporate logos saturate our world, echoing each other to absurd degrees, producing a semiotics of symbols that need little or no commentary. In arguing that literature is indeed alive and well, and in calling for a renewed examination of its place in the world, Szeman and O'Brien feel obliged to cite Michael Hardt and Antonio Negri's 2000 book *Empire*, which highlights the diffusion of capital and its power, one that supersedes anolder operation of empire defined by national boundaries. Today, by contrast, as *Empire* argues, global capital is virtualized, freed from territorial restrictions. If Hardt and Negri are too quick to celebrate the death of the nation-state (which, as current events constantly remind us, are very much alive), the authors are right to mention that a key feature of our globalized world is language. No wonder that many of today's noteworthy novels—Amitav Ghosh's *The Shadow Lines*, Zadie Smith's *White Teeth*, Aravind Adiga's *The White Tiger*—accentuate a world that is ever more mixed, culturally, racially, and linguistically.

To be sure, globalization is not new. Greek coins have been found in India, artists from different cultures have always copied each other's work, and several ancient cities are remembered as crossroads for cross-continental trade. When Vasco da Gama came into Calicut five centuries ago, he had the help of an Indian pilot whom he discovered in Arabia. Clearly, "discovery" is a relative term in this context. Nor is globalization an evaluative term—or rather, it should not be. I agree with Amartya Sen (in *The Argumentative Indian*) and others that, for better and worse, the global exchange of goods and ideas has profoundly shaped human history.

What *is* new about this phenomenon is the intensification of global trade and social relations, and the omnipresence of media. Some have called this the McDonaldization of the world, a view that *New York Times* columnist Tom Friedman has long championed. Others have been less charitable, coining such terms as "coca-colanization." Regardless of our views of this complex development, there is no doubt that we now live in a very different world than existed even fifteen years ago. This world, more than ever before, is structured and defined by economics. Where does literature fit in? While my interest in this topic—that is, the place of literature in a world increasingly defined by Sensex and Dow Jones averages—stems from my teaching of post-colonial literature in the U.S. and my upbringing in India, I have lately noticed a similar concern among students in my literature classes. The local, to expand on the opening lines of this essay, are increasingly hard to disentangle from the global. Students increasingly notice that novels, poems, plays and essays depict a changing world, and that these same texts are themselves part of the commodification, or marketing, of art. (I often discuss blurbs on the jackets of new novels to prompt a discussion of how such packaging intersects with cultural values and politics.) I need not remind readers that a corporate, economically-driven model of governance is now dictating the mission of education around the world. Presidents of many universities in the U.S. now add the acronym CEO to their title. The idea of the university as a sphere of unrestricted thinking, and the bedrock notion of a well-rounded education, are in jeopardy. It is worth citing here Amartya Sen's reminder that this ideal of the academy was alive and well in the ancient Buddhist university of Nalanda. It is not simply a European ideal. This seems especially important for students in the west to understand.

Globalization and Narration

As we have seen, scholars like Szeman and O'Brien, and including Marshall Berman in his discussion of Orhan Pamuk's novel *Snow*, have recently called attention to possible ways in which the rise of globalization and the corresponding diminishment (ostensibly) of the nation-state will affect the literary imagination and its readership. These developments are said to especially pertain to the novel, that amazingly successful, free-form bourgeois expression of individual and social desires. On the other hand, as Gikandi and others have noted, nationalism is alive and well in its political and cultural forms. Even the so-called "world novel" by writers as diverse as Achebe, Garcia Marquez, Rushdie, and Pamuk, and which the critic Franco Moretti has championed, cannot, as Gikandi makes clear, do without the "framework of the nation." Gikandi rightly observes that the world novel, and the profession of English studies in particular, in fact depends for its success on an interpretive community of readers and scholars who, despite different nationalities and generations, nonetheless all share a "postcolonial" education that ironically owes much to its colonial inheritance. These writers and thinkers, in other words, share a surprisingly similar postmodern sensibility.

To return to my original question, therefore: How do we reconcile the global and the local, the national and the global, coloniality and postcoloniality, as these relate to both the novel and our pedagogical interests? To a great degree, the so-called world novel owes its success to the continued influence of the European languages in which it is written—despite the fact that, as this audience knows much better than me, regional, non-European vernaculars have a rich history of their own that do not appear on critical radars in New York or Paris or Madrid, and that do not depend on what these radars indicate. On the other hand, the hyper-globalized world in which all novels now appear (and, some would say, become commodified) means that there is a trans-national sensibility which these novels express and to which they respond—a sensibility that is not simply about the clubbishness of elite institutions, but which reaches to all corners of the globe. To try to address these questions, I will glance at some novels in order to support the following provisional contentions: The narrative of the novel—and narrative in general—has always been global, though never more so than now; the teaching of literature and concomitant questioning of "canonical" texts reflect the on-going changes occurring in literary studies; and cultural and regional identities must, as result, be open to revaluation. I mean that by reading literature comparatively, in a global context, students learn to define themselves not simply according to nationalist or religious or urban ideologies, but by means of a dialogic, constantly negotiated web of standpoints. This may seem to advocate merely a decentered, a moral, quiescent reading of texts and of history. This is why our reading must begin from an ethically committed stance—a stance that, in fact, virtually all noteworthy literature advocates. In one sense, then, this active, as opposed to passive, reading of literature challenges us to understand its ethical core.

One constant in the interpretation of fiction has been the split between the "country and the city", as the Marxist critic Raymond Williams phrased it in his influential study of that name. Similarly, the Indian social critic Ashis Nandy has called attention to the dominance of cosmopolitan ideologies over "alternative", non-urban ideas. But while this split has certainly been true on a broad level from the industrial revolution and colonialism down to our times, it does not help us very much in discussing the contemporary novel. In some ways, we are all caught in the world wide web of a mass technocratic society. These splits occur at countless levels, or what Arjun Appadurai has called "disjunctions". Appadurai argues that although nationalists frequently rebel against the intrusion of global capital, most familiarly by attacking brand names that are perceived to diminish home-grown values (such as attacks on McDonald's in different countries), the line between seemingly innate "tradition" and outside "modernity" constantly shifts. Even as the flow of capital depends upon a level of uniformity that can threaten cultural differences, it is also compelled to rely on its local market, which is why corporations are increasingly sensitive to local concerns. Some, like Arundhati Roy and Vandana Shiva, rightly point to the ethical void that purely economic interests encourage. Others, like economist Jagdish Bhagwati and the aforementioned Friedman celebrate the supposed "flatness" of today's world, and many talk these days about the Internet's democratizing tendencies.

Curiously, this for-or-against argument about globalization in some ways resembles past arguments about the novel. Frankfurt School critics from the 1940s through the 70s generally held the arts responsible for getting caught in the "culture industry" and of forgetting the aim of truth. If Hollywood was the sign of sameness and loss of critical awareness, bourgeois novelists were held accountable for having cashed in on their ethical imperatives. More recently, critics inspired by Foucault have argued that the novel, far from being a medium of truthfulness, in fact participates in the complicit in "policing" the bounds of middle-class propriety—in other words, that the novel conditions our values.

An alternative view was earlier presented by the Russian critic Mikhail Bakhtin, who saw in the novel's intrinsic dialogism a democratizing force that enabled previously silenced members of society, including women and children, to gain a voice in the conversations about civil society. (This explains why Soviet authorities bullied Bakhtin into silence for the next four decades.) And although Walter Benjamin, a friend of some of the Frankfurt School members, was speaking about photography and cinema in his essay on "mechanical reproduction," his premise that the ability to reproduce art at least allows it to be shared by all, rather than only the elites, can be applied to the novel as well.

In sum, globalization is seen as either an enabler of individual expression or of manufactured consent, just as the novel has been viewed as alternately a tool of bourgeois repression and as a voice for the voiceless. What, then, are we to conclude? My own view lines up with Bakhtin's. In relation to globalization, I suggest more specifically that the novel long ago provided us with a model of what a globalized yet emancipatory vision should look like. Just as Appadurai posits that disjunction and difference in today's McDonaldized world can enable unique voices to flourish, and just as Bakhtin champions the intrinsic "heteroglossia" and polysemy of the novel, so do I believe that the novel, which ironically depends for its sale on generic resemblances and commodification, nonetheless provides us with truly unique expressions of individuals and societies that are responding to a changing world. Perhaps this is not surprising. After all, literature is all about disjunction and paradox and ambiguity, and language is perfectly suited to the cumbustible nature of the world it depicts. An apt metaphor of this is Dickens's character Krook in *Bleak House*, who spontaneously combusts—an emblem, perhaps, of the obsessive, meaningless hoarding that modern society can induce in its alienated inhabitants.

Consider a recent, tragicomic novel that ponders the implications of a rapidly transforming world, Aravind Adiga's *The White Tiger*. The voice of the narrator-protagonist, Balram, is a naïve one in the classic mold, the narrative winking at the reader whilst the narrator is clueless about the implications of his own words. The entire novel is, of course, in the guise of a letter to the Chinese premier. It's interesting in this regard to consider what features of India Balram believes are important to highlight. More telling is the language Balram uses, including his nickname the "white tiger", which he earns in primary school when a teacher in his village calls him the smartest in the class, a "white tiger", for he is "the rarest" of jungle creatures. Shortly thereafter, however, Balram is forced to work in a teashop as part of his father's debt.

Later, when Balram escapes his village to follow the lure of the big city, he is first mystified and then angered by the talk he overhears between his boss, Mr. Ashok, and Ashok's wife Pinky Madam. He says that they "talk about India, about America—mixing Hindi and English together" (47). Here, language marks class, much as it does in the novels of Dickens and Twain. Indeed, Balram's own effort to learn English and ultimately write letters to the Chinese leader illustrates the linguistic stakes involved in today globalized world. Perhaps most telling in this regard is Balram's statement early in the novel that "Iqbal...is one of the four best poets in the world—the others being Rumi, Mirza Ghalib, and a fourth fellow, also a Muslim, whose name I've forgotten" (40). This replays the ironies in which Balram is caught: a driver who is a poet, a city-dweller in modern India who looks to poets of a different age, an Indian who feels compelled to write to the premier of the country now seen to be India's arch rival in trade. It also reveals Balram's innate love of language. He is, as the novel shows, a close and savvy student of words. For all his worldly-wise motivations, Balram intuits the truthfulness of poets, how their words encompass worlds. Balram's own language, indeed, is frequently poetic, as in his refrain to Delhi: "Speak to me of civil war" (220). There is no indication in the book, and it seems unlikely, that Balram reads Urdu. He has memorized these poets, which demonstrate their oral influence. His fondness for ghazals and street knowledge of English together reveal that his worldview is just as hybridized as that of his rich boss, though in different ways.

How, then, does Balram's poetic sensibility coexist with his turn to violence? Bakhtin provides a partial answer: Not only is Adiga's novel populated by many voices, Balram's voice itself is ambivalent, composed of competing desires and obligations. He is at once proud of his nation and angry with it; he has a clear sense of guilt for what he's done (which in fact leads to the novel-length letter itself as a kind of confession), yet also exults in having avenged the many injustices he has experienced. Whatever his actions, Balram clearly possesses a sense of right and wrong that he normally pretends to ignore. Balram's ambivalence is, I would say, one that many people in today's world experience. The commodification of desires in today's global village, whatever else it may do, certainly engenders a contradictory range of sentiments within individuals. These characters face existential dilemmas no less acute than those faced by Camus's Meursault in *The Stranger* seventy years ago. But in many ways, I would argue, characters like Balram are more recognizable to more readers today than Camus's protagonist could ever be—largely because Balram, like us, is bombarded by images that continually beacon to him, images that promise him (and us) a bigger piece of the cultural and economic pie. Balram's fatal decision to knife his boss amplifies Meursault's decision to pull the trigger that kills a stranger. But in an environment like Balram's Bangalore, where everyone seems to be simultaneously familiar and estranged, his final choice is less meaningless and more recognizable. The choice has, in other words, an ethical quotient that rebels against an indifferent world.

I think we can connect the contradictory allegiances and desires to the very paradoxes of the world—or worlds—we today inhabit. Amartya Sen has said that "There is, in fact, no real conflict between being determined to resist global inequality and injustice and at the same time understanding and facilitating the positive contributions of globalized economic, social and cultural relations across the world." If Balram is able to see a larger world than anything his village forebears could have imagined, it is largely due to the country's changed conditions in a time of globalization, a change that simultaneously promises a more comfortable livelihood and an ever greater potential for unscrupulous behaviour.

Conclusion

Balram's enchantment with and reliance on language is recognizable for other reasons. We are, for instance, familiar with the linguistic turn in the humanities, beginning in the late 1960s, and including a wide array of disciplines and scholars. We are also familiar with hybridity in the public sphere, as in Spanglish (Spanish + English) and Hinglish. (In Sri Lanka, I saw an amusing play that was equal parts English, Sinhalese, and Singlish. It was very popular; I wish I understood it.) We are familiar, too, with Englishized Hindi, as in the following translation: "Hot [haat] sexy image wali Priyanka romantic role key sath abb filmo me action [yekshun] aur stunt bhi karna chahti hai." Such code-switching needs no gloss in India, just as a Spanglish radio station would not need one in Miami. Given that urbanites across the globe are accustomed to these new creolizes, we should ask ourselves and our students how this relates to literary representations. What class markers can we detect, what desires and motivations, in such code-switching? Such questions are, I believe, directly connected to the reasons we turn to literature as a means of making sense of the world.

A novel from a generation previous to Adiga's may be an instructive one with which to conclude. Nayantara Sahgal 1969 *Storm in Chandigarh* ponders the implications of India's modernization, women's roles (especially), and the very idea of freedom. Sahgal, like many others, posits that a nation is not truly free unless all its citizens are given the opportunity to life and liberty. What interests me in regard to our theme is the reflections of Sahgal's protagonist, Dubey, a young, idealistic IAS officer sent to Chandigarh to sort out a labour dispute that unfolds against the backdrop of the then-recent division of Haryana and Punjab states. It is no accident that a central theme in the book is communication (or its lack)—between couples, between politicians, and ultimately between the political class and ordinary citizens. Dubey, who at one point says that he really wishes to be a writer, is the classic outsider, one who observes, chews on, and digests the actions of those around him, while keeping in mind the ultimate purpose behind the whole experiment of nationhood. Sahgal point here, among others, is that nations are conceived as narratives, and that they demand constant re-imagining, particularly in a nation like India where tradition and modernity collide in the ways Appadurai outlines. Fittingly, the setting for the novel is Le Corbusier's brand new, planned city of Chandigarh. The theme of modernity is unavoidable, and Sahgal wishes to underscore this with her title. "Storm" means different things, from the "storm" rising within the restless character of Mara to that of the strike to political tensions. But the most significant storm, it seems to me, is the dispute over India's path. As Sahgal's uncle, Prime Minister Nehru, noted in *The Discovery of India*, the challenge for India was to balance its ancient heritage with its new form as a nation-state. Four decades after Sahgal's novel, with India's transformation galloping along far faster than Dubey could have imagined, Adiga's Balram is still trying to balance his own aspirations with those of his nation and of the globe.

REFERENCES

Achebe, Chinua. *Home and Exile*. New York: Anchor Books, 2000.

Adiga, Aravind. *The White Tiger*. New York: Free Press, 2008.

Appadurai, Arjun. "Disjuncture and Difference in the Global Economy." *Public Culture*, 2:2 (Spring 1990): 1-24.

Berman, Marshall. "Orhan Pamuk and Modernist Liberalism." *Dissent* (Spring 2009): 113-18.

Damrosch, David. "World Literature in a Postcanonical, Hypercanonical Age." In Haun Saussy, ed., *Comparative Literature in an Age of Globalization*. Baltimore: Johns Hopkins University Press, 2006. 43-54.

Fishkin, Shelley Fisher. *Was Huck Black?: Mark Twain and African-American Voices*. New York: Oxford University Press, 1994.

Gikandi, Simon. "Globalization and the Claims of Postcoloniality." *South Atlantic Quarterly*, 100:3 (Summer 2001): 627-58.

Hardt, Michael and Antonio Negri. *Empire*. Cambridge, MA: Harvard University Press, 2001.

Nandy, Ashis. *The Intimate Enemy: Loss and Recovery of Self Under Colonialism.* Delhi: Oxford University Press, 1983.

O'Brien, Susie and Imre Szeman. "Introduction: The Globalization of Fiction/ the Fiction of Globalization." Special issue on globalization, *South Atlantic Quarterly*, 100:3 (2001): 603-26.

Sahgal, Nayantara. *Storm in Chandigarh*. Delhi: Penguin, 2008 (1969).

Saussy, Haun, ed. "Introduction." *Comparative Literature in an Age of Globalization*. Baltimore: Johns Hopkins University Press, 2006. 43-54.

Sen, Amartya, *The Argumentative Indian: Writings on Indian Culture, History and Identity*. New Dehi and London: Penguin, 2005.

Steger, Manfred. *Globalization: A Very Short Introduction*. New York: Oxford University Press, 2009.

❑❑❑

Odysseus: The Ancestor of 'The Wandering Crusoe'

RAMA KUNDU

> Vain search for one island that heals with its harbour
> ....There are so many islands!
> As many islands as stars at night....
>
> –Derek Walcott '*The Schooner* Flight'

> Now the sea is the Argonaut's sea, and in the dawn
> Odysseus calls the commands, as he steers past those foamy islands
>
> –D.H. Lawrence 'The Argonauts'

THE shipwrecked sailor-narrator in Marquez's *The Story of a Shipwrecked Sailor* (1970) claims towards the end, it has been "my odyssey" (Marquez 105). What he learns to his pleasant surprise is that the story of shipwreck and the subsequent struggle, survival and final landing still excites interest and stirs some sympathetic chord lying hidden in the listener's deep psyche, even in this era of advanced media exposure. As Velasco relates his real-life 'odyssey' to avid listeners, he realises

> how much interest the newspapers had in the story of my ten days at sea. Everyone was interested. My own friends asked me to tell it many times. (Marquez 105)

It is the ageless appeal of the age-old story of struggle and survival of a hapless individual in the face of formidable nature that accounts for the 'interest' evinced by Velasco's listeners:

> It never occurred to me that a man could become a hero for being on a raft ten days and enduring hunger and thirst...in my case, heroism consisted solely of not allowing myself to die of hunger and thirst for ten days. (Marquez 101)

> ...all day and all night, whatever the circumstances, people want to hear you talk about yourself. (Marquez 102)

At the same time, the shipwrecked narrator also speaks from a compelling urge. On being asked by the first man, 'what happened to you',

> I realized that more than thirst, hunger, and despair, what tormented me most was the need to tell someone what had happened to me. (Marquez 92)

Therefore, he assumes the narrator's role, much like Odysseus in palaces and royal halls in remote isles amidst strange perilous seas.

The *Odyssey* indeed constitutes the foundation of the endlessly repeated and infinitely layered archetypal tale of sea voyage-shipwreck-survival. The very word, 'Odyssey', has become in course of centuries a term and loaded sign, as it has gone on acquiring newer and newer layers of meanings, of connotation and signification, to subsequent poetry, drama, fiction, travelogue, the arts (including painting, sculpture, music), to which it still continues to send tentacles across the world.

"The *Odyssey* is less severe in structure and focus than the Iliad" (Kirk; 'Intro' viii). The reason is obvious. It is the tale of wandering. Like Kirk, Steiner also complains of a lack of focus in the *Odyssey* in contrast to the tight structure of the *Iliad*: "A marvel of design and variousness, but difficult to get into focus" (Steiner; 'Introduction' 9). But the very nature of the content of the narrative—a voyage narrative as it is—necessitated the apparent 'diffuseness'; indeed Steiner himself seems to suggest the cause when he comments: "Like the sea water which laps its every page, the vision of the poem is swift, changing, exploratory, prone to odd shallows and sudden depths" (Steiner; 'Introduction' 9).

The Odyssey seems more a tale of islands than of the sea. It is a long sea-voyage punctuated by so many island stops. Apart from the main islands we also find casual mention of quite a few other minor isles: for example, Book Four ends with Penelope's suitors planning to kill Telemachus; with this target they set forth "and sailed water-ways as far as a stony island in mid-sea, equidistant from Ithaca and craggy Samos, even the islet Asteris, no large place: which has a harbour with two approaches and in it a berth for ships. Thus, they drew up to lie in wait for him" (trans. Shaw 54). John Fowles, in his book *Islands*, indeed perceptively observes the intimate link of western narrative with island journeying, as he refers to the successive island landfalls of the *Odyssey*, each of which constitutes a chapter or 'Book' in the tale (Fowles 51).

"The geography of the tale is a riddle. It appears to include Greece and Ionia, Crete, Lycia, Western Sicily, Egypt, and even a hint of Mesopotemia. At times, it is clearly a geography of the imagination, bristling like medieval maps with fables beasts and wind-daemons blowing out of every quarter" (Steiner; 'Introduction' 9). Steiner further comments: "what is inescapable in the Odyssey is a sense of the oriental" (Steiner; 'Introduction' 10).

As a narrative of wide wandering, "The Odyssey's action moves over three separate landscapes" (Kirk; Intro viii): Ithaca, the Peloponnese, and the mythical or fantasy islands. Here is the order of the places our hero—Sisyphus, Peregrine Picaro, Robinson Crusoe, Gulliver rolled into one—visited: Ismarus, home of the Cicones; Island of the Lotus-Eaters; Island of the Cyclopes; Aeolia, home of Aeolus; Aeolia for a second time; Telepylus, the stronghold of Lamos, home of the Laestrygonians; Aeaea, home of Circe; the Underworld; Aeaea for a second time; the Sirens; Scylla and Charybdis; Thrinacia, home of Helios' sacred cattle; Scylla and Charybdis again, (Odysseus' raft got sucked into the whirlpool Charybdis); Ogygia, home of Calypso; Scheria, home of the Phaeacians; finally Ithaca, the journey's end.

According to one school of opinion, the lotos eaters were on the *island* of Jerba, as opposed to the North African coast. Calypso's island was called Ogygia. The Siren's island is called Sirenum Scopuli. The lotos island is called Island of Lotos-Eaters.

Anyway, what emerges to be of much more importance is that the *Odyssey* is a tale of long suffering, and final triumph, corresponding to a pattern (now turned archetypal) of long wanderings which finally end in homecoming. "The Trojan War itself had been bad enough, but Odysseus' real sufferings came in the ten years that followed, which he spent in wandering and hardship before finally regaining his island home in Ithaca..." (Kirk; Intro vii). This is the "main narrative theme" (Kirk; Intro vii). But within this broad pattern, the epic is in a way a string of island narratives, which together present a series of narrativized islands. Imaginary places as they are, the poet has presented most of them through the narration of a character, who is supposed to have been in these remote spots, and subsequently imparting his first-hand experience. It is a kind of oral reportage, flavoured though with the narrator's personal response, as well as reminiscence,—a kind of 'emotion recollected in tranquility'. Thus these turn out to be narratives at a second remove, or micro-narratives within a metanarrative. These are co-ordinated by, as well as focused on, a single hero.

Book I of the *Odyssey* opens with the invocation: "Goddess of song, teach me the story of a hero. This was the man of wide-ranging spirits who had sacked the sacred town of Troy and who wandered afterwards long and far. Many the troubles that vexed his heart as he sailed the seas, laboring to save himself and to bring his comrades home…" (Trans. Shewring 1). Indeed, Odysseus' adventures and growth are indisputably more foregrounded in the epic than that of any other character. It is owing to this that the sea-beaten old voyager is the hero, and not the young Telemachus, howsoever enterprising and impressive he might have proved himself to be. G.S. Kirk, an admirer of Homer as he is, registers the point with a slight disappointment as he compares the *Odyssey* to the *Iliad*. "Scores of Iliadic fighters…come alive, if only for a line or two; the poet imagines them as a people, with a home and a living background, and this turns their death or their moment of triumph, into something more than a mere statistic of warfare. This simply does not happen in the Odyssey: Odysseus's crew in the adventures, even the demoralized Eurylochus, hardly exist except as a necessary group, labouring or complaining, weeping or expiring as events demand" (Kirk 1962: 367). Even Telemachus remains shadowy, in comparison,—as Aragon would sense at the other shore beyond the ocean of centuries; in Louis Aragon's modernist novel, *The Adventures of Telemachus* (1922) the young hero implores Calypso from behind the shadow of his absent father, without reference to whom his own image fails to take shape: "Madam, …could you look without pity on a youth in quest of himself throughout the world, for indeed…my father ceaselessly carried far away from me by the very same *fury of tempests and concepts* that thrusts me naked at your feet" (12-13; emphasis added)? However, one can guess, the poet perhaps needed this unifocality, as the canvas here is made to incorporate endlessly shifting spaces lying across almost immeasurable watery lengths and breadths, instead of a single city and battleground. Furthermore, apart from the author, it is Odysseus who happens to be the single narrator, directly delivering his strange island experiences in his own voice.

The first eight books are in the third person narration or the authorial voice. From Book Nine to Book Twelve Odysseus takes over as the narratorial voice, rendering the various phases of his sea-voyage, from island to island, in the role of an oral narrator addressing and catering to an island king and his court. On occasions he attains a remarkable degree of self-distancing, as the [is] landed oral narrator Odysseus looks back to the voyager Odysseus, struggling to get free from some magical or terrible captivity, or desperately negotiating with the wild gong-tormented sea. Book Thirteen gives the last leg of the journey. In Book Fourteen he arrives at Ithaca, the destination island. Even after reaching Ithaca, he has to tide over some forbidding obstacles before he can finally celebrate his homecoming. From Book Fourteen to Book Eighteen we have the third person narrator's account of this last encounter with fate, rendered in the form of linear narrative.

In the island ruled by king Alcinous Odysseus is received with honour. And it is here that he begins his act of narration, at the instance of the queen: "It is grievous for me, O Queen, to give you a connected history of my pains. The celestial gods have given me too many. Yet this I will say to meet your questioning. There is an island, Ogygia, lying afar in the ocean..." (trans. Shaw 77).

Indeed, "the connected history" of his pains is but the string of island-tales which are connected by the thread of the hero's suffering. So it is only appropriate that he should immediately embark on his narration with the sentence: "There is an island...lying afar in the ocean..." (Shaw 77).

Incidentally, Marquez's first person narrator also concludes: "I have *told* my story on television and on a radio program. I've also *told* it to my friends. I *told* it to an elderly widow with a huge photograph album who invited me to her home" (Marquez 106; emphasis added). The repetition of 'told' suggests the performance of an oral narrator to an eager audience. Still some people would insinuate, 'this story is a fantasy'; to which Velasco snaps back: "If it is, then what did I do during my ten days at sea?" (Marquez 106).

In the ancient epic, it is this direct transmission of the oral delivery on part of the castaway hero, which lends a particular vividness and veracity/authenticity to a tale which continuously weaves between realism and fantasy, and frequently slips into the latter realm, which, following the literary triumphs of Borges, Marques, *et al.*, seem to lay claim to the title/domain of 'magic realism'.

Fantasy

Human imagination, at that early stage of sea-voyaging, was naturally prone to envision the farflung remote islands in the far-off seas as domains of fearsome fantasy, rather than coveted and vanquishable virgin land, and to fantasize them accordingly. Though Odysseus does not have to fend for himself, like his later-day successors in the various desert islands of colonial fiction, his islands are not less dangerous than the colonial islands, but rather much more fraught with dangerous, even deadly lures, traps, threats—infested as these are with superhuman and subhuman creatures, including man-eating giants, who can pose greater threat than the life-size cannibals of later day European travelogues. Some of them have the added ability to metamorphose a human into a subhuman, and vice versa. Odysseus's experiences in these isolated spots, lying scattered like so many seeds on the map of endless and bottomless seas, are usually more misadventures than adventures.

T.E. Shaw, who is more generally known as T.E. Lawrence, had suggested in his 'Translator's Note' to "the twenty-eighth English rendering" of Homer's *The Odyssey*, that Homer was probably "a book-worm, no longer young, living from home, a mainlander, city-bred and domestic".

Shaw/Lawrence also slyly put in the idea: "Perhaps the tedious delay of the climax through ten books may be a poor bard's means of prolonging his host's hospitality" (Shaw 3).

He conceded, however, "few men can be sailors, soldiers and naturalists", and claims furthermore: "Yet this Homer was neither landlubber nor stay-at-home nor ninny. He wrote for audiences to whom adventures were daily life and the sea their universal neighbour. So he dared not err" (Shaw 2).

Anyway, any reader today knows that these tales are at best instances of magic realism, so far have these 'brain-bred' islands been removed from factual/actual reality; yet the charm of the narration is indeed so irresistible that the reader has no difficulty in attaining 'willing suspension of disbelief' even after so many centuries. In the words of G.S. Kirk: "It is the tale of that complex and inspired man, amid the confused aftermath of the Trojan War, in lands remote from the Ionian coasts where Homer sang, or even at times from prosaic reality in any form, in an amalgam that contains much of what the Greeks continued to feel and to believe..." (Kirk; 'Introduction' xx).

It is indeed a fantasy world and also a fantastic world; indeed more comparable to Gulliver's fantasy islands, with its super-realistic flora, fauna and inhabitants including demons, fairies, witches, giants, as well as lotos-eating, siren-hooting specimens of *homo sapiens*.

Fantasy Island: Tropes

Odysseus's islands have eventually emerged not only as legendary places, but archetypal tropes, loaded signs—be it the Lotos-eators', or the Sirens', the land of Circe, or that of Cyclopes, etc.

Odysseus narrates, how after being driven across the seas by "ravenous winds" for nine days they made the land of the 'Lotos-eaters', Tennyson superbly reenacted the episode, along with its mood of rich languishment in his poem by the same title. In the afternoon they come to a beautiful land of perpetual afternoon; against the 'rosy flame' of the 'charmed sunset' "the mild-eyed melancholy Lotos-eaters came" (Tennyson 24). People here are not aggressive or hostile, instead they offer a dish of flowers, feeding upon which "all memory of home fades" (Shaw) from the taker's mind; or is it the will to return which fizzles out? In Tennyson's poem the sailors having tasted the lotos are seen to slip into a dreamlike impassive condition.

> …sweet it was to dream of Fatherland,
> Of child, and wife, and slave; but evermore
> Most weary seem'd the sea, weary the oar,
> Weary the wandering fields of barren foam.
> Then someone said, 'We will return no more;'
> And all at once they sang, 'Our island home
> Is far beyond the wave; we will no longer roam'. (Tennyson 25)

Odysseus has to drag his people back on board and immediately embark again. This is a fantasy island, where the terrible prospect is catered under cover of a charming garb. It is the very lure of rest and relaxation, which paradoxically makes him scared, because this would make him forget the destination which he cannot allow himself to forget. Incidentally, during the voyage Odysseus does not seek rest; instead rest is forced upon him on certain isles, clamped as it is by divine design.

The next stop looks idyllic, but this is only an illusion. It is "a fertile island, a wooded island" close to the Cyclopes' place. It is a solitary pastoral island, full of goats. It is fertile soil, offering the promise of restful life, and full harvest.

> Anything would grow well there in season, in the soft moist meadows behind the dykes of the silvery sea: and its vine-stocks would bear

> for ever. The crop to be harvested at the due time from such smooth plough-loam would be heavy.... Its haven is a natural port requiring no such gears as anchors or warps. (trans. Shaw 93-94)

But it is flanked by the habitation of the terrible cannibalistic monster, Cyclopes, who devours part of the crew. Odysseus has to take on him.

The next stop is the Aeolian island, the splendid palace of Aeolus, the 'keeper of winds' "in that sea-cradled fastness, within a bulwark of invincible bronze from which the cliff falls sheer" (Shaw 103). It is a danger-free fantasy zone—an epitome of generous hospitality; but all the positive fruits of the hospitality are squandered away, owing to the greed of the crew. After happily staying there for one month the crew set sail once again, equipped with Aeolus's parting gift, a leather bag with all the strong winds tightly packed inside. After sailing nine days and nights, while home seems almost accessible, the greedy crew unfasten the bag in the hope of gold, and disastrous winds bore them off. They manage to return to Aeolian island, but this time there is no reception; instead they are thrown away with disgust as objects of the gods' disgust.

So sailing out again, this time gloomily and with hard labour as there was no helping wind like the former time. The next stop is again a fantasy island, but it is the fantasy of horror. "Its harbour is good, for an unbroken rock shelters it from side to side...inside the haven there was never any swell...but a white calm constantly prevailed" (Shaw 104).

The calm is only apparent. The peace is only an illusion. Before long they realise it is a land of the giant cannibals, and have to flee in horror before all of them were swallowed down.

> "the stout Laestrygons, not human-looking creatures these, but giants. They gathered missile stones each a man's weight and cast them down on us off the cliffs" While thus smashing the ships and men, "the natives were busy spearing my people like fish and collecting them to make their loathsome meal" (trans. Shaw 105). [Is it foreshadowing Gulliver/Rabelais?]

Incidentally, it may be noted that in course of the voyage he repeatedly loses ships and mates, and always with the same and only consolation, parenthetically mentioned: "(yet with the consolation that we were still alive)".

They stop only after reaching another island, the island of Æaea, ruled by Circe. It is a "land-locked harbour", which they float into. It is an "ample landscape" (Shaw 105) as he finds out from his look-out rock. As he recounts his reporting to his fellows:

> I climbed the hill to look out, and saw that this is an island which the limitless sea encircles like a wreath. The island itself is flat and my eyes perceived how in its heart smoke rose from the midst of a dense wood. (trans. Shaw 106)

This is another charming isle, yet containing potential danger, under cover of its charming appearance, which would surface before long. It is only through the hero's tact and prowess that his trapped companions are eventually saved. After the visit to the Underworld, or the House of the Dead he comes back for a brief stop to Circe's island once more. The next stop would be Thrinacia, and the last challenge would be greed. Prior to this would be the Siren's island, another fantasy island [underpinning the terrible lure of the fantasy] which they will quickly pass by, as advised by Circe:

> Your next land-fall will be upon the Sirens.... The thrilling song of the sirens will steal his [the listener's] life away, as they [the sirens] sit singing in their plashet between the high banks of mouldering skeletons which flutter with the rags of skin rotting upon the bones. (trans. Shaw 126)

They call "Hither, come hither"; we know all things that happened and will happen.

Gabriel Germain's interesting argument: "The Homeric Sirens have no exact mythological shape or nature…. The Sirens promise knowledge; *who has heard them leaves 'knowing more'*. To Odysseus, whose name they know without having questioned him, they would speak willingly of the heroes of Troy, but they also have knowledge 'of all that comes to pass on the fruitful earth'. Thus, the bait they hold out to a circumspect mind is that dread fruit of knowledge for the sake of which our first parents lost Eden. Whatever the blandishments to which the Sirens may resort when dealing with mariners of a coarser breed, *it is this alone by which they seek to ensnare Odysseus*" (Germain 92). Germain claims: "In restoring its full significance to this temptation *through knowledge*, we remove this brief narrative from the sphere of naïve parables and relate it to a body of myths of which we have just cited the clearest and best known" (Germain 92-93). Again, indeed, "the temptation of a hero by some evil power which seeks to make him betray his essential destiny, seems to be an ancient Sumerian theme" (Germain 93). Germain concludes: "it is noteworthy that on every hand a study of the Sirens leads outside the confines of the classic world" (Germain 98).

Kafka's amused conjecturing on 'the silence of the Sirens' is an interesting instance of one of the many varied ways this island—seen through a distant swift fearful glimpse only—has stirred bright minds across ages and lands.

Both Tiresias in the Underworld, and Circe had forewarned them:

> Yet have you a chance of surviving to reach Ithaca, despite all obstacles, if you and your followers can master your greed in the island of Thrinacia, when your ship first puts in there for refuge from the lowering sea, for in that island you will find at pasture the oxen and wonderful sheep of Helios our Sun. (trans. Shaw 115)

Apparently this is also another magic realistic place. Dire disaster followed as anticipated. After drifting for nine days he came to Calypso's island, from where to Alcinous's. Alcinous arranges for his last safe trip, to Ithaca at last, though in disguise.

The islands throw up so many obstacles to homecoming: some in the form of potential destruction—directly by cannibals, or indirectly through metamorphosis inflicted by witch craft—but mostly in the form of lure of various shades. It can be the lure of avarice (gold), of greed (meat), of knowledge (Sirens), of sweet rest (Lotos), of luxurious comfort (Circe), of perpetual comfort, pleasure, along with the prospect of immortality capping all (Calypso). Lure proves to be a much more formidable force than other direct forms of captivity and hindrance. The message conveyed through all these micronarratives is: 'Go ahead, wandering mariner, until you reach home'. One great fear is the fear of being stranded.

Contrapuntal to these realms of fantasy is the home island, which is rendered in realistic terms, and located in real-life geography and society. The mist of mystery is lifted as the hero reaches Ithaca.

The Home

The theme of a real home and real homecoming looms large over this fantastic travelogue.

The Odyssey opens *in medias res*, in Ogygia, a "far western isle" ruled by Calypso, the sea nymph. Here Odysseus has already been held captive for seven years, by the nymph, with the promise of immortality on the condition of his staying on. Yet even such a lure cannot quench his longing for home and family, which again is located in yet another island. So, the voyage of Odysseus through the sea and the varied islands, is actually a journey to Ithaca, a nostalgic return journey towards the final destination island, the home, a very very prolonged journey, stretching over years, challenging, hazardous, frequently interrupted, but never completely abandoned. It is his intense longing for home which indeed constitutes the basic motivation behind the endlessly hazardous, frequently frustrating journey. This is what has eventually made the name 'Ithaca' emerge as a loaded sign.

Home

Home, Sweet Home!:

When the island happens to be one's own home:

In course of the voyage, Odysseus drifts from island to island, rejecting each one that comes on his way, until he reaches one last island, that is his home.

The multilayered concept of 'home' and 'homelessness' have been increasingly taking front stage in social discourses as well as literary praxis in our times.

Home has been so many things to so many people simultaneously, as well as across ages! One tends to recall Eliot's definition, albeit one-sided: he points out in East Coker V, 'Home is where one starts from'; with no less validity one can also argue, it should signify the point where one would come back, or at least long to come back, at the journey's end; thus paradoxically, it is the point of departure as well as the point of last arrival, or final return. Again, this idea of last arrival can be contested by the proverbial philosophical pessimism—'you can't return home'.

In Jean Rhys's *Voyage in the Dark* (1934) the heroine in exile in the unaccustomed cold continent misses home, and remembers an island "all crumpled into hills and mountains as you would crumble a piece of paper in your hand—round green hills and sharply-cut mountains." She dreams: "I was on a ship. From the deck you could see small islands.... And the ship was sailing very close to an island, which was home except that the trees were all wrong. These were English trees, their leaves trailing in the water. I tried to catch hold of a branch and step ashore, but the deck of the ship expanded (Rhys 140).

In his wonderful fantasy tale 'At the Auction of the Ruby Slippers' in [*East, West* (1994). London: Vintage Books, 2007] Salman Rushdie writes:

> 'Home' has become such a scattered, damaged, various concept in our present travails. There is so much to yearn for. There are so few rainbows any more. How hard can we expect even a pair of magic shoes to work? They promised to take us *home*, but are metaphors of homeliness comprehensible to them, are abstractions permissible? Are they literalists, or will they permit us to redefine the blessed word? (Rushdie 93)

In the same story a 'condemned man on another planet' is mentioned, who had been sent off to Mars but cannot return owing to abrupt cancellation of space exploration budget. The Martian sings on TV, some medley of half-remembered songs including "Show Me the Way to Go Home…" (Rushdie 97). The lonely narrator conjectures that once he gets hold of the magic slippers, he might win back his lost love: "Perhaps I might even click the heels together three times, and win back her heart by murmuring, in soft reminder of our wasted love, *There's no place like home*" (Rushdie 98).

Odysseus recounts "the tale of the calamitous *homeward* journey with which Zeus had afflicted my return from Troy" (trans. Shaw 92). It is calamitous, but nevertheless set for "home" all the time. At the start of his narration introduces himself, with particular reference to his own place, his home-island.

> I live in pellucid Ithaca, the island of Mount Neriton, whose upstanding slopes are all a-quiver with the wind-blown leaves.... *My island* stands deep in the sea.... It is a harsh land...*but perhaps in every man's sight there is nothing better than his native land.* (trans. Shaw 91)

Looking back upon his own experience he finds further confirmation of his assumption: In spite of being offered exquisite new homes promising endless comfort by Calypso and Circe respectively, he cannot forget his longing for Ithaca. "Wherefore I say that no matter how rich a man's circumstances may be abroad, among foreign parts, there is no sweet in life to compare with home and parents" (trans. Shaw 92).

In Calypso's island he should have been satisfied, at least on material counts, i.e., including all physical needs and comfort. Yet he was not happy, because of his undrowned longing for Ithaca.

Having been received well by Alcinous, Odysseus implores the king: "to scheme how you may put this unlucky, toil-worn self of mine ashore in the land of my fathers. Let life leave me then—so that my dying eyes behold my property, my men, and my wide stately house" (trans. Shaw 77). He also expresses wish "that when this cruel spell is past I may become your host in my house—my very distant house, alas!" (trans. Shaw 91).

After the lapse of one full year in the comfort and pleasure of Circe's place, Odysseus's men succeeded in persuading him by means of reminding him of 'home'. "Master, it is time you called to memory your native land, if fate will ever let you come alive to your well-built house and ancient estate" (trans. Shaw 111).

Homecoming

The Sirens epitomise the lure of the alien, another obstacle/hindrance to homecoming. Circe warns Odysseus; "If a man come on them [the Sirens] unwittingly and lend ear to their Siren-voices, he will never again behold wife and little ones rising to greet him with bright faces when he comes home from sea" (trans. Shaw 126).

Ithaca at last!

One of the archetypal sequences in world's literatures.

When he reaches Ithaca at last he cannot believe he has really arrived home, so great and repeated had been the thwarting of all expectations of reaching home ever. Then at last "the joy of seeing his place so wrought upon Odysseus that he fell to kissing its bounteous soil" (trans. Shaw 142). We are again transported from the fantasy world to the real world of real geography.

Just as Ulysses cannot recognize Ithaca even after reaching the home-island, so longed for, Marquez's Velasco, the hero of an actual even of shipwreck, reaches homeland without realizing it.

I don't know why, but I thought I was somewhere in the Caribbean other than Colombia (Marquez 92). He asks the man watching him, 'What country is this?'

> And very matter-of-factly he gave the only answer I wasn't expecting at that moment: "Colombia". (Marquez 93)

Castaway

Perhaps, psychologically too, Ithaca is the only real place in the hero's perception/consciousness, whereas the rest might as well be so many "brain-bred islands" (*à la* Elizabeth Bishop's 'Crusoe in England'), where the sea-beaten, scarred, devastated Odysseus had arrived, or perhaps imagines he had arrived, as an outcast or castaway, an ancient pre-figure anticipating, in a remote way of course, another famous literary castaway at the turn of another later age. Thus, he is also in the long line of castaways, a forerunner actually; in a way, preceding them by ages; yet carrying an unmistakable mark of the family likeness. He is the original of an archetype, that would ensue in a later era—the archetypal figure of 'the Wandering Crusoe'.

Of course there is a major difference; once landing on the isle-shore he did not have to fend for himself like his less illustrious successors; because those were not the desert islands of English/European literature of the imperial/colonial era, which would prove to be so fascinating and challenging for the imperial generations, who would come to a far off island, by chance or design, in order to annex it to the empire. Having no such colonial programme of 'marvellous possession' (*à la* Greenblatt) up his sleeves,—since the discourse of imperialism was apparently unknown to Homer—Odysseus would be continuously on the run all the time, escaping from island to island, escaping from one island, launching out on the sea, only to be captured or to get bogged down in yet another, in an almost endlessly repetitive, frustrating Sisyphean process. Instead of being a conqueror, or possessor, he comes to the islands as a compulsive suppliant, a fugitive from sea-hazards, but before long seeks to flee it desperately as an escapee captive. He has no intention to settle down, nor annex it to an empire like the patriarch of 'The Family Robinson' , like the boys of Ballantyne,—his many textual successors on so many trctual/actual islands in the South Pacific, or the Caribbean, or round the equatorial belt.

In yet another sense Odysseus is an early forerunner of the resourceful, trickster Picaro hero, coming so very much ahead of his time, scraping in and out of countless traps; the traps are laid out on the islands, which turn out to be fertile ground for spawning off countless unforeseen and unpredictable challenges.

The Castaway

In course of the epical voyage there is a reminder about another terrible homecoming: Agamemnon laments to Odysseus in the House of the Dead: "I was coming home, promising myself the joyous greeting of my children and my household: and then she, by the depth of her villainy... (trans. Shaw 121-22).

The counter-point to homecoming is being castaway.

As a tale of islands, it is perhaps only natural that the castaway figure should loom large. The castaway had already been the signifier for the man who can take the challenges of life, howsoever hard those might be. The castaway figure called up in the listeners' mind pity, terror, admiration, respect. It also set him thinking about the causes, the forces behind such events, obviously divine forces.

As Hermes, Zeus's messenger reaches Calypso, carrying Zeus's message to her to release Odysseus, the nymph says resentfully: "Yet it was I who saved him as he clung astride his vessel's keel, alone and adrift in the wine-dark ocean Zeus had launched a white thunderbolt at his ship and shattered her: and in her wreck were all the worthy henchmen lost. Only it chanced that he himself drifted to my shore before the wind and waves" (trans. Shaw 57).

Anyway, like Crusoe Odysseus has to make his own raft himself, working for four days at a stretch, though he is given the material by Calypso. Having found his release from Calypso's island, Ogygia, Odysseus sets for home again, but is again shipwrecked on the Phaeacian isle. Before long this raft will be shattered in the wide sea and he be cast ashore, "a fugitive" (Shaw 63) from the wraths of the sea-god. But myths apart, his physical sufferings are as rudely real as any castaway's.

> ...a huge wave flung him upon the rugged shore. There would his flesh have been torn off and his bones shattered had not the goddess Athena prompted him to seize[d] the rock in both hands. (trans. Shaw 63)

Crusoe would have done the same in a similar situation, though without any Athena to prompt him.

> To it he held...until the force of the wave passed him by...but afterwards the backwash enveloped him and cast him once more into deep water. Exactly as when a squid is dragged out from its bed the many pebbles come away in the suckers of its arms, so did

> the skin peel off Odysseus's strong hands against the stones. Then the billows closed over his head. (trans. Shaw 63)

After reaching the shore with tremendous effort

> Odysseus's knees gave way together, and his sinewy arms: for his reserve of manhood had been used up in the long fight with the salt sea. The flesh had puffed out over all his body and the sea water gushed in streams from his nostrils and mouth...and terrible was the weariness which possessed him....
>
> Then Odysseus struggled up from the river, to collapse in a bed of reeds; there he embraced the fruitful earth.... (trans. Shaw 63-64)

Is it too different from the experience of the shipwrecked sailors of Defoe, or Swift, Ballantyne, or Stevenson, or even as late as Gabriel Garcia Marquez? It is the eternal lone individual negotiating with eternal nature in the raw. After ten days' drifting in the wide sea, Marquez's Velasco nears the shore:

> With tremendous effort, I managed to push ahead to where it was only up to my thighs. Then I decided to crawl. I dug into the sand with my hands and knees and pushed myself forward. But it was useless; the waves pushed me back. The tiny sharp grains of sand abraded the wound on my knee. My fingertips were scraped raw.... I could feel the sand penetrate the flesh under my fingernails... [Driven by] tremendous energy—a vitality born of terror—and painfully, without mercy for my raw fingertips, I went on crawling against the force of the undertow.... Ten minutes later...I lay exhausted on the warm, hard beach, not thinking about anything, not thanking anyone, not even rejoicing.... (Marquez 88-89)

The extraordinary moment of landing is a common experience shared by all wrecked sailors down the ages. These are comparable to Odysseus's several landings, particularly the last one before Ithaca.

> What a strange sensation it was to touch the ground after drifting at sea for ten days. (Marquez 88)

Driven by

> a vitality born of terror...painfully, without mercy for my raw fingertips, I went on crawling against the force of the undertow. Ten minutes later, all the suffering and hunger and thirst of ten days took their toll on my body. I lay exhausted on the warm hard beach, not thinking

> about anything, not thanking anyone, not even rejoicing that, by force of will, hope, and an indefatigable desire to live, I had found this stretch of silent, unknown beach. (Marquez 89)

This is perhaps the crux of all shipwrecked castaways' tales. It is the 'gripping' and reassuring story, the good old story of survival, which never fails to excite and charm.

Robinson Crusoe's first-person narration brings us to a moment not too different: "the sea having hurried me along as before, landed me, or rather dash'd me against a piece of a rock, and that with such force as it left me senseless.... Seeing I should be cover'd again with the water, I resolv'd to hold fast to a piece of rock..." (Defoe 49). After finally landing: "I believe it is impossible to express...what extasies and transports of the soul are, when it is so sav'd...out of the very grave" (Defoe 50).

Gulliver's ship, driven by a violent storm, dashes against a rock and is immediately split. "I swam as Fortune directed me, and was pushed by Wind and Tide." Reaching the shore he was "extremely tired...lay down on the grass, where [he] slept sounder than ever" in his life (Swift 35). Thus, he arrives at the Liliputs' island. In Ballantyne's 19th century bestseller, near 'the coral island' a gale wrecks the ship by dashing it upon a rock, only the three boys survive the struggle in the wild sea, and arrive at 'the coral island' as outcast (Ballantyne 7).

Prior to reaching the island of King Alcinous, "As his [Odysseus's] raft breaks apart beneath him it means determining to stay alive despite everything, and carefully weighing up the position—exactly what to do as one is swept toward a rocky shore—with the decisive practicality of a professional soldier or sailor" (Kirk; Intro xix). This is an experience that Odysseus undergoes over and over again, playing the realistic role of a real-life expert sailor, yet continuously sailing along in and out of a realm of magic and fantasy as a Sisyphean castaway.

Discourse: Themes

Spiritual Growth

In 'Hidden Themes from Homer's Odyssey' Brian Lower, Chad Croley, Jeremy Fine, and John Kelley have respectively traced the following four underlying themes from the Greek culture in this narrative: spiritual growth, loyalty, perseverance, and hospitality.

"*what doesn't kill us makes us stronger.*"

> It is his long voyage, punctuated by the many island stops that corresponds to a kind of *bildungshroman*. This is perhaps one of the multifaceted messages that can be derived from the *Odyssey* even today. Brian Lower holds: "Homer uses the idea of spiritual growth as one of his underlying themes in the Odyssey. He relates this message through various characters and their adventures or actions. Spiritual growth is brought on by rough times, temptations, long travels, and even good times. Homer does a good job of hitting on all of these factors".

Lower further argues: "Telemachus also experiences spiritual growth, but Homer displays it in a different manner. Whereas Odysseus' growth is concerned with situations, Telemachus' is dependent upon a journey. He is sent away from home in search of his father. It seems as though the prince was so dependent on his father that he never really got away from home on his own. It took his father's disappearance to force Telemachus into a leadership role. He visits friends of his father's and experiences 'xenia' as the normal head of households do. Through his journey, he learns to depend on the gods and returns home a more spiritually inclined man. Telemachus learns how to make decisions and trust the instinct that the gods give to him."

Brian Lower concludes:

> Homer shows many different types of spiritual growth throughout the Odyssey. But, he has one main idea: the spirit with the most growth and strength is the one that is tested and weakened through the process. Telemachus' spirit grows, but cannot compare to that of Odysseus because he was not weakened and tested as much as Odysseus. The weakening allows a person to grow stronger, not just grow. ('Hidden Themes from Homer's Odyssey')

Discourses: Themes

Loyalty

> The ancient discourse regarding the issue of loyalty was not obviously the same as that of the modern discourse. Although it is not uncommon to apply modern insights and modern concepts to ancient classics, one cannot afford to lose sight of the original context.

Chad Croley's exposition seems to offer a case in point. Croley explores the theme of loyalty in *The Odyssey* from a feminist angle. Croley maintains:

"Loyalty has to be seen as a major theme in and can be seen as having a significant meaning to Odysseus's story." She therefore proposes to "discuss the idea of how Odysseus's loyal supporters still remain devoted to him even after he has been away for nearly two decades as well as pose a question pertaining to Odysseus's own actions of infidelity" and pose "a question to be thought about", by citing the instance of Penelope's patient devotion through the long years of separation from husband, and contrasting it with Odysseus's unfaithfulness vis-a-vis his wife. She holds brief for Penelope and rather resentfully accuses Odysseus:

> Penelope is shown as the most loyal of all by staying faithful and true to her husband even though they are not together. She resists time and time again the attempts of the suitors for her hand in marriage. So, why is it that Odysseus is so unfaithful to his wife? He is unfaithful with at least two characters Circe, whom he stays with for a year and Calypso, where he is held captive for seven years but sleeps in her bed. Of all the characters that are so loyal to Odysseus, why is he so unloyal in return? ('Hidden Themes from Homer's Odyssey')

Penelope's extraordinary devotion and constancy are indeed legendary; Eumaeus, Odysseus's loyal swineherd, also remains faithful and committed to the master. He boldly tells Odysseus, who is in disguise at the time: "I call him my lord, although he is not here". Telemachus too, as a son, is so devoted as to undertake a voyage to learn more about his father. The two together stand by him through the ensuing trouble with the suitors.

Croley holds that Odysseus has proved disloyal to those who have been devoted to him, including Penelope, as well as Circe and Calypso, with whom he had betrayed his faithful wife. Anyway, this is apparently a feminist angle, which obviously did not hold sway in the continuum of the *Odyssey*. Furthermore, it would be rather unfair not to mention that Odysseus climbed the bed of Circe, in accordance with the explicit advice of Hermes of the gold rod:

> your best suit is not to spurn this divine paramour but to make the lying with her a lever to free your followers and win kindly treatment for yourself. (trans. Shaw 108)

The norms and values of those times were different, and apparently not gender-oriented.

On the other hand, according to Jeremy Fine, both Odysseus and Penelope are examples of great perseverance which is sustained through crises and challenges over long years. Indeed, in a particular sense, Odysseus remains loyal; it is loyalty to the home and the home [is] land.

Divine Discourse

However, the dominant discourse that governs the epic is the Divine discourse, as the Greeks would have accepted and subscribed to in those days. Odysseus begins his act of narration, at the instance of the queen of Alcinous: "It is grievous for me, O Queen, to give you a connected history of my pains. The celestial gods have given me too many" (trans. Saw 77).

In course of this journey there was the chance of death at every turn, but for the grace of Athena, the goddess who continues to guide him and save him from total destruction. Why should she save him, and yet allow him to suffer so much and so long! The answer to this riddle lies in the Greek view: "We suffer to grow wise". Every ordeal leaves him wiser and stronger. Thus the actual voyage, the island intervals alternated by the churning in the wild sea, is accompanied by a parallel process of a spiritual growth turmoil, crises. However, the whole thing—his suffering as well as his final return—is governed by "divine decision" (Kirk; Intro x), as the Greek would believe. It is the Olympian decision, followed up by active divine intervention. Even as the hero is bogged down in the comforts of Calypso's captivity, "the singer takes his listeners straight to Olympus, where the gods debate Odysseus' fate and decide that he should be allowed to return home" (Kirk; Intro x). Accordingly Hermes is sent to Calypso, and Athene herself descends in disguise to prepare Telemachus. The original listeners of Homer apparently did not question the veracity or authenticity of the report or explanation.

E.V. Rieu in his 'Introduction' highlights "that galaxy of Olympian gods whom the reader is faced with at the very beginning of the poem and will meet as individuals on almost every page" (Rieu; 'Introduction' xv). Rieu challenges the assumption that Homer's attitude is detached and sophisticated. "He does believe in his gods, and that very vividly, but…regards his gods, though immortal, as made in the image and likeness of man. Mixed with his deep respect for their almost unlimited powers and his aesthetic appreciation of their beauty, he betrays a very tolerant understanding of their motives and frailties.... But it was neither flippant nor irreverent. These powerful beings, who were so intimately connected with men's passions and desires, were there to administer, not necessarily to obey, man's moral code. Christian apologists of a later age made a mistake when they suggested that the pagans had invented the gods and their iniquities as an excuse for themselves. Homer never censures a god nor lets a mortal use a god's misdeeds as a pretext for his own" (Rieu; 'Introduction' xv).

Rieu also touches the subject of Homer's 'artistic use' of the superhuman realm: "The most casual reader must at every page be struck by the contrast between the carefree happiness of the Olympian company and the toiling, anxious world of men. This contrast is woven into the very texture..., and is nowhere turned to better account than when Odysseus refuses immortality as a gift from Calypso" (Rieu; 'Introduction' xv).

Camps comments on the 'pagan view' of the world operating in Homer's deliberations. "Supernatural powers are at work everywhere and always in the Homeric poems, causing things to happen which modern man would suppose to be due to known material causes, or human character, or simple chance" (Camps 8). Camps points out: "An incidental result of this way of seeing and explaining things is that the difference between the probable and the improbable is less strongly felt than it is in a world in which human or material causes are assumed to be responsible for most events and luck responsible for the rest" (Camps 8).

Camps offers an interesting sidelight in this connection:

> From this conception of the gods as human in form and mentality (though superhuman in power and exempt from the human destiny of death) there results a perspective which sets the quality of the human agents in relief. Because of their nearness to and converse with the gods the heroes are seen—as 'men such as now men are' cannot be—as peers of the gods themselves in strength and splendour. Because of their mortal condition they acquire—as carefree and immortal gods cannot—the moral dignity of effort and endurance. This sense of the kinship and contrast between men and gods illuminates the poet's picture of his heroic world. (Camps 9)

Odysseus is a mortal man, and his sufferings and joys are those of the mortal human. Thus the very theocratic discourse can be deconstructed to highlight an underlying anthropocentric vision.

[Incidentally, The hero of the *Ramayana*, although a mortal incarnation of the divine, yet undergoes the most acute sufferings of a mortal man, as a resentful son, a husband whose wife has been snatched by a lustful person, a bereaved husband, a bereaved brother] Steiner would have us "...take the only fully explored relationship in the Odyssey, the friendship of Athene and Odysseus. The goddess and the Wanderer delight in virtuosities of deception. They...bargain like street merchants of Damascus, seeking to outwit one another with affectionate larceny" (Steiner; 'Introduction' 11). At one point Athene lovingly mocks him:

> Enough of such speaking in character between us two past-masters of these tricks of trade—you the cunningest mortal to wheedle or blandish, and me, famed above other gods for knavish wiles. (trans. Shaw 140-41)

[unlike the arrogant and capricious deities of the *Iliad*] "the flavor is oriental" (Steiner; 'Introduction' 11).

But the suggestion of parity between the mortal and the immortal, even when the case in point is a minor deity, is ruled out by Kirk:

> He is a survivor who fights his way home to take up life again where it should be taken after war: among one's own people, surrounded by the possessions one has fought for, and solaced by the wife who is one's partner.... That at least what the Greeks of the heroic tradition believed in.
>
> To achieve all that, Odysseus has to hold firmly to the past...to what he knows himself to be. With Calypso, that means above all remembering that he is mortal, a social being, not destined for solitary love with a creature of another kind. (Kirk; Intro xix)

Indeed, the *Odyssey* begins and ends respectively with reference to divine talk about mortals' fate, and divine intervention in the mortals' action. In the end as Odysseus is about to come down upon the suitors "like a swooping eagle", Zeus lets fly a flaming bolt, and "Athene called out at once to Odysseus...commanding him to hold his hand...for fear of offending the ever-watchful Zeus" , and thus "established peace between the two contending forces" (trans. Rieu 351).

Camps holds: "Nevertheless, the war is thought of fatalistically as a visitation sent by the gods on men, part of the inevitable sorrows to which man is subject" (Camps 69). Indeed repeatedly characters tell this to one another,—Priam to Helen, Achilles to Priam, Odysseus to Agamemnon.

King Alcinous tells Odysseus as he grieves over the minstrel's song: "That was wrought by the Gods, who measured their life's thread for those men, that their fate might become a poem sung to generations yet to be" (Bk 8, trans. Shaw 91).

"To odysseus" (*odyssasthai* in Greek) means "be wroth against", "hate", "planting evils", " be causer of pain". In the First Book Zeus says that excessive suffering is due to folly. This prompts Athene to ask: "but what about Odysseus? Why do you odysseus him so, Zeus?" George E. Dimock comments: "It is a good question, and it contains its own answer. In exposing Odysseus to Poseidon, in allowing him to do and suffer, Zeus is odysseusing Odysseus, giving him his identity" (Dimock 121).

Indeed, infinite layers of meanings can be attributed to, or traced in, the epic. But one wonders why did the poet have to place his tales in the far-flung, and obviously unreal, islands in order to project themes which are supposed to be so commonly and reverentially held by his people? Does it seem a bit puzzling?

Theme: atonement: humane discourse

The blood and tears of sacked Troy had to be washed by the sea-water; atonement for the blood-bath had to be made through repetitive immersion (baptism) in the sea-foam, through bathing by the salty waves.

W.A. Camps comments:

> The *Odyssey* looks back with grief and regret to the war at Troy, notwithstanding the victorious outcome of that war, to which the *Iliad* looks forward.... The surviving victors Nestor and Menelaus are thinking always of their fallen friends.... But even in the Iliad, though there is joy of battle as well as agony, and admiration of warlike skill and courage, there is no glorification of war as such. The war is seen by men on both sides as a calamity visited on them by fate or gods, and the victories...are told as hollow triumphs for the victors. (Camps 3-4)

Odysseus himself, a victor, weeps most disconsolately at the recounting of the event. At King Alcinous's palace the minstrel sings of the fall of Troy (Book VIII). While listening to the song, "Odysseus melted and tears…bedewed his cheeks. So it is when a loving wife flings herself, wailing, about the body of her man who has fallen before his township and fellow-citizens, defending the town and his children from their cruel day of sack and rapine. The sight of him laboring his last breath and dying makes her wail aloud and wind herself herself about him. Yet do the enemy from behind beat her with their spear-shafts across her bowed shoulders and lead her into servitude, to her fate of toil and grief. Just as that woman's cheeks are ravaged with despair, just so piteously did the tears fall from Odysseus' brows" (trans. Shaw 90).

> "Already in the Iliad, Odysseus marks a transition from the simplicities of the heroic to a life of the mind more skeptical, more nervous, more wary of conviction. Like Odysseus, Homer himself abandoned the stark, rudimentary values inherent in the world of Achilles. When composing the *Odyssey*, he looked back to the Iliad across a wide distance of the soul.... In the *Odyssey* gleam the first dawn light of the Socratic future" (Steiner; 'Introduction' 14).

Point counterpoint: Islands and Home: Conflicting pulls?

Home is sweet. The home-island is the last dear destination. Still, the attraction of the remote mysterious islands cannot be denied. Odysseus the castaway, arriving at Calypso's fragrant isle can be compared to Jibananda Das's shipwrecked speaker arriving at the fragrant island of 'Banalata Sen'. When Hermes "at last...attained that remote island", he found the nymph's hearth-fire perfuming the island far across with the fragrance of flaming cedar-wood logs and straight-grained incense trees" (Shaw 55).

Furthermore this place is one of idyllic beauty with its "luxuriant copse of alder trees and black poplars and rich-scented cypresses: therein roosted birds of long wings. A young strong vine with bunches of grapes wreathed the opening.... Four springs jetted out transluscent water.... The soft lawns were starred with parsley and violets" (Shaw 55). No wonder even an immortal like Hermes should pause before such beauty and feel glad; and Tennyson's Ulysses, after reaching home through untold sufferings yet again should long to sail out once more. The perennial dichotomy between 'home' on the one hand, and call of the wild, distant, isolated spots on the other!

The 'lotos'-eating sailors' choric song underpins another dimension of the dichotomy between the [is] land and the sea, the opposite pulls of the repose on land and the challenge of the sea, in which the former seems to be stronger than the latter on occasions at least.

Surely, surely, slumber is more sweet than toil, the shore
Than labour in the deep mid-ocean, wind and wave and oar;
Oh rest ye, brother mariners, we will not wander more

('The Lotos-Eaters', Tennyson 28)

Ithaca, which has become synonym for homecoming, has also acquired a host of richly ambiguous and conflicting meanings, some of which are touched upon by 20th Century Greek poet C.P. Cavafy's poem "Ithaka": how Ithaka has come to mean so much and so many things to 'voyagers' in the sea of life:

When you set out for Ithaka
ask that your way be long,
full of adventure, full of instruction.
The Laistrygonians and the Cyclops,
angry Poseidon—do not fear them:
....
................—you will not meet them
unless you carry them in your soul
unless your soul raise them up before you.
....
Have Ithaka always in your mind.
Your arrival there is what you are destined for.
But do not in the least hurry the journey.
Better that it last for years
....
Ithaka gave you the splendid journey.
Without her you would not have set out.
She hasn't anything else to give you
....
So wise have you become, of such experience,
that already you will have understood what these Ithakas mean.

(Cavafy 158-59)

WORKS CITED

Aragon, L. The Adventures of Telemachus. (1922) [trans. R.R. Hubert & J.D. Hubert]. Lincon: University of Nebraska Press.

Ballantyne, R.M. *The Coral Island*. London: Abbey Classics. n.d.

Camps, W.A. *An Introduction to Homer*. Oxford: Clarendon Press, 1980.

Cavafy, C.P. "Ithaka". in *Homer: A Collection of Critical Essays*. [Eds. Steiner, G. & Robert Fagles] N.J.: Prentice-Hall, Inc., 1962.

Defoe, D. *Robinson Crusoe*. Kolkata: Rupa & Co. (by arrangement with W. Collins, London), 1989.

Dimock, George E. Jr. "The Name of Odysseus" in *Homer: A Collection of Critical Essays*. [Eds. Steiner, G. & Robert Fagles] N.J.: Prentice-Hall, Inc., 1962.

Fowles, J. *Islands*. London: Cape, 1978.

Germain, Gabriel. "The Sirens and the Temptation of Knowledge" in *Homer: A Collection of Critical Essays*. [Eds. Steiner, G. & Robert Fagles] N.J.: Prentice-Hall, Inc., 1962.

Homer. *The Odyssey*. [trans. by T.E. Shaw] (1932). Hertfordshire: Wordsworth Classics, 1992.

Homer. *The Odyssey*. [trans. by Walter Shewring]. Oxford: OUP, 1980.

Kafka, Franz. "The Silence of the Sirens" in *Homer: A Collection of Critical Essays*. [Eds. Steiner, G. & Robert Fagles] N.J.: Prentice-Hall, Inc., 1962.

Kirk, G.S. *The Songs of Homer*. Cambridge: Cambridge University Press, 1962.

——. 'Introduction' to *The Odyssey*. [trans. by Walter Shewring]. Oxford: Oxford University Press, 1980.

Lower, Brian, Chad Croley, Jeremy Fine, John Kelley. "Hidden Themes from Homer's *Odyssey*" (2002).

Maequez, Gabriel, G. *The Story of a Shipwrecked Sailor.* (1970). [trans. from Spanish by Randolph Hogan], rpt. London: Penguin Books, 2014.

Rhys, Jean. *Voyage in the Dark* (1934). London: Penguin Books, 1969.

Rieu, E.V. 'Introduction' in Homer: The Odyssey [trans. E.V. Rieu] (1945) London: Methuen & Co. Ltd., 1952.

Rushdie, Salman. "At the Auction of the Ruby Slippers" in *East, West* (1994). London: Vintage Books, 2007.

Shaw, T.E. 'Translator's Note' to Homer's *The Odyssey*. [trans. by T.E. Shaw] (1932). Hertfordshire: Wordsworth Classics, 1992.

Steiner, G. "Introduction: Homer and the Scholars" in *Homer: A Collection of Critical Essays*. [Eds. Steiner, G. & Robert Fagles] N.J.: Prentice-Hall, Inc., 1962.

Steiner, G. and Robert Fagles [eds]. *Homer: A Collection of Critical Essays*. N.J.: Prentice-Hall, Inc., 1962.

Swift, J. *Gulliver's Travels*. Kolkata: Rupa & Co. (by arrangement with W. Collins, London), 1989.

Tennyson, A. *Selected Poems*. London: Penguin Classics, 2007.

❑❑❑

Frankenstein or the Modern Prometheus, the 19th Century Sci-Fi: A Critical Overview

ADITI BHARDWAJ

Introduction

PUBLISHED in 1818, *Frankenstein or the Modern Prometheus,* brought in a lot of fame and appreciation for Mary Shelley. Not only because it is said to be the first Gothic fiction, but also as it proved itself to be a product of an age which began rapidly chasing for more and more progress in science and advancements in technology. Although, it is quite possible that even Mary Shelley did not intend to write the novel as the first science fiction because it was the result of a ghost story telling contest between Mary, her husband Lord P.B. Shelley and Lord Byron in Switzerland. So Mary also busied herself "...to think of a story.... One which would speak to the mysterious fears of our nature and awaken thrilling horror—one to make the reader dread to look around, to curdle the blood, and quicken the beatings of the heart" (ix-x). One day, listening to the conversations between Lord Byron and Shelley about various philosophical doctrines, nature of principles of life, Darwin's theory of 'Origin of Species', etc., she began to think that life cannot be conferred upon by man but a corpse could be reanimated through the principles of galvanism and similar theories. It was on that night that:

> I saw...the pale student of unhallowed art kneeling beside the thing he had put together. I saw the hideous phantasm of a man stretched out.... His success would terrify the artist; he would rush away from his odious handiwork, horror-stricken. He would hope that, left to itself, the slight spark of life...would fade...subside into dead matter.... He sleeps; but he is awakened...behold, the horrid thing stands at his bedside, opening his curtains and looking on him with yellow, watery, but speculative eyes. (Shelley, xi)

Thus, herein we find the source of this hideous but trend-setting gothic fiction because she thought that "what terrified me will terrify others;

and I need only describe the spectre which had haunted my midnight pillow" (Shelley, xi). So, possibly she did not think that the story of an irrational scientist, which she plans to pen down to horrify others, will actually claim the position of being the first science fiction.

Robert Walton, on his voyage towards the North Pole, saves a man named Victor Frankenstein whom he finds in a wretched condition surrounded by ice. Victor narrates his story to Robert that being interested in Natural Sciences and occult mysteries he gets obsessed with the desire to create life. He attempts to animate a human frame but actually creates a hideous giant creature whom the people and he himself assume to be a monster. This creature initially looks for a company as it is abandoned by its creator himself, but when the doors of the entire humanity is shut on its face, it pursues Victor to take a revenge by devastating his life and family. It is then that Victor follows the monster with murderous intentions but breaks down due to the unbearable cold and is taken on board by Walton. After the death of Victor, the monster pledges not to show its face to humanity ever again and disappears behind the snow-covered mountains.

There are various *themes* which Mary has directly or indirectly touched upon. The novel seems to be overtly praising *advancement of science and technology* as the titular character is obsessed with reading and applying various scientific theories and principles. But, at the same time, it also seems to be talking about *the limits of the use of science and technology* as Victor faces the consequences of blind pursuit of the same. She emphasises on *the constructive as well as destructive powers of science*. The story also leaves a vast scope of the interpretations of the *concepts of humanity and monstrosity*. Victor makes a collection of dead disproportionate limbs stand alive but he himself behaves so inhuman towards it that the polite and love-craving creature turns into a revengeful and heartless monster. Both of them seem to be in diametric opposition of each other because his *ambition*, *selfishness* and his *inhuman behaviour* towards his own creation entitles him more for the title 'monster' as compared to the creature. If the creature is hideous by appearance, Victor is hideous in his acts and hence, most of us recall the name 'Frankenstein' as that of the monster rather than its creator because we associate monstrosity with the name of the heartless character and not with the ugly creature. Victor, who tried to *imitate God's art of creation*, failed drastically in his aim because God loves the entire humanity irrespective of the fact that a person is normal or differently—abled but Victor first accumulated limbs and parts from dead bodies, infused a spark of life into it through principles of theories like galvanism and then detested and disowned his own creation. She discusses that *blind pursuit of knowledge* can be dangerous as Victor attempts to surge beyond the accepted human limits to discover new secrets of life. The parable also emphasizes upon the concepts of *family, relationships, emotions, sentiments, love, companionship* and *society* through Victor's family especially his caring father, selflessly loving mother and Elizabeth, the love of his life. The monster initially chases Victor for the sake of companionship as he is suffering from loneliness (*man is a social animal*) and tries to be friends with the de Lacey's family but on being detested from everywhere and everybody starts hating humanity. He longs for a companion but when his plea is rejected by Victor his anger and hatred towards him shoot up. The story is also about the *sense of responsibility, right and wrong, good and evil, inner peace, revenge,* etc. Victor's blind pursuit of his ambition makes him stay away from his relationships and lose his health and his wrong deeds and *guilt* drive him towards his *death*.

As a science fiction, the narration also possesses the themes of *artificial intelligence* which is represented by the monster as a *replicant* of human being. The creature also serves as an example of *cloning, bio-implant* or *body/genetic modification* as Victor uses parts of dead bodies to create a human frame. The monster is able to bear any type of climatic conditions (possibly because of the disproportionate body parts) which touches the theme of *life extension, immortality,* and *artificial organs.* When on the demand of the monster, Victor decides to create a female companion for the former, the latter shudders with the thought of their progeny which gives a slight hint of the *race of the future.*

Shelley here gives the *message* that scientific and technological developments are necessary for the improvement of human life but if they are not pursued in the proper directions, they can even worsen the human conditions for nothing can stand against the natural phenomena. Playing with science without any prior thoughts to the after effects of the experimentation, we invite danger for our own lives. This message is quite relevant today also, be it artificial genetic creation of animal or as all the countries are racing in the production of nuclear power but once used it will affect the entire humanity.

Frankenstein falls into the category of *Soft* SF because its focus is not so much upon the scientific rigor. Though the climax builds up due to the use of scientific elements in the story, it emphasises more upon the importance of family, relationships, emotions, friendships, companionship, love, hatred, revenge, sacrifice, etc. It can also be categorised as a *Dark SF* as it makes use of the features of a science fiction but also employs gothic and horror elements which keep the readers shivering with fear in their seats. *Frankenstein* as an early nineteenth century novel could create a place of its own in the ocean of English literature because Mary Shelley knew as an author the appropriate amount of science and literature to be blended to make the nineteenth century readers fall in love with it. And it still holds relevance for readers as well as critics today.

Shelley has aptly used the ancient Greek myth of Prometheus in the backdrop of the Romantic age and the title *Frankenstein or the Modern Prometheus* is relevant in the present context also. Prometheus was a Titan God of forethought as his name suggests and he was entrusted with the responsibility of creating mankind. One version of the myth says that Zeus, the supreme Greek deity of thunder, had taken away fire from man and for the betterment of his own creations, Prometheus stole fire from Zeus and gave it to humanity. Another version says that Prometheus cheated the Gods during a meal by sacrificing worst parts of animal offerings to them and keeping the best edible parts for humans to feed upon. Due to this, Zeus took away fire from mankind so that they eat raw meals and created Pandora, the first woman to send misfortune and misery into the human being's house. In both the cases, Prometheus enraged Zeus through his acts and as a punishment for his betrayal with the Gods, he was chained to a rock and his liver which re-grew every night was fed upon by an eagle everyday. After scores of years, he was rescued by Heracles from his continuous torment. By calling Frankenstein, the modern Prometheus, Shelley intends to say that like Prometheus, Frankenstein tried to give something to humanity but it had drastic consequences for him as well as for humanity. And as punishment for his ill-directed and blind pursuit of ambition and for disobeying God's will, his guilt fed like the eagle upon his inner peace everyday till he passed away chasing his creation.

The concepts of creator and creation are a little complicated because they are woven intricately with one another. When the creator abandons his creation, the newly-born creature longs for somebody (at least his creator) to share his loneliness in this world like a parent, guardian, caretaker and companion. On being refused for support, shelter and a female companion, the creature develops hatred towards Victor and kills Victor's entire family clan. Victor chases it with murderous intentions but gets himself killed due to the unbearable weather and climatic conditions. So the creator creates this creature but finding it detestable tries to kill it, however, to the readers' dismay and surprise, it is the creation which drives its creator to his death.

Victor Frankenstein is the main character of the novel. He is the titular hero as well as a doomed protagonist as he initially struggles to achieve his ambition of knowing the secrets of heaven and earth and then his ambition costs him his life by the end of the novel. He is the narrator of the main portion of the story to which Robert Walton and his crew members on the ship are the listeners. He represents that section of the society which is selfish, unreasonable, ungrateful, irresponsible, coward and can cross any limit to achieve name and fame.

We are introduced to *the creature/monster* in the IV chapter (Volume 1) when Victor makes it stand alive through his experiment. He is described as eight foot tall, an ugly and hideous creation of Frankenstein which has yellow eyes, yellow skin, lustrous black hair, pearly white teeth, straight black lips, gigantic stature and detestable countenance. Intelligent and sensitive, the monster quietly observes the de Lacey's family and tries to learn the rules of human society. He tries to approach everyone for companionship and stretches out a friendly hand, but all those who see him shun him. His abandonment compels him to seek revenge against his creator and with the death of his creator, he disappears into darkness.

Robert Walton is the Arctic seafarer whose letters mark the beginning and the end of the novel *Frankenstein*. He aspires to tread the road not taken yet. Since his sister, Margaret, was not in favour of his expedition trip, he writes her letters regularly about his safety and well being. Walton nurses Frankenstein back to health and hears his story which is the main story of the novel. He records the incredible tale in his letters and encountering Victor's death on board drops his plan of sea adventure and returns back home taking a lesson.

Margaret Saville is a passive character as she is only mentioned as the recipient of Walton's letters.

Alphonse Frankenstein is Victor's father and is an example of kindness and selflessness. He is a good husband and a very loving father. He dies of the pangs of misfortune of his family seeing each one of them falling in distressful situations one by one.

Elizabeth Lavanza is an orphan, four to five years younger than Victor, whom the Frankensteins adopt. The family wants Elizabeth and Victor to marry each other when they grow up. She represents true passion, love and an ideal womanhood. She eventually marries Victor (for which she waited entire life) but is killed by the monster on their wedding night.

Henry Clerval is Victor's boyhood friend, who nurses him back to health in Ingolstadt. He is the first one to be killed by the monster but the police arrests and accuses Victor for his murder.

William Frankenstein is Victor's youngest brother and the darling of the Frankenstein family. The monster strangles William in the woods outside Geneva in order to hurt Victor for abandoning him.

Justin Moritz is blamed and executed for William's murder, which was actually committed by the monster.

Caroline Beaufort is the daughter of a merchant friend of Victor's father. After her father's death, Caroline is taken by Alphonse Frankenstein as his wife and becomes Victor's mother. She dies of scarlet fever, which she contracts from Elizabeth.

There is a family of peasants including a blind old man de Lacey, his son and daughter, Felix and Agatha, and a foreign woman named Safie. The monster learns how to speak and interact by observing them. When he reveals himself to them, hoping for friendship, they beat him and chase him away.

M. Waldman and *M. Krempe* are professors at the Ingolstadt University where Victor studies. *Mr. Kirwin* is the magistrate who accuses Victor of Henry's murder.

There are some passive women characters in the novel, which are doomed to remain silent or suffer till their deaths. Margaret Saville is given the identity of only being the recipient of Walton's letters. Caroline Beaufort becomes abandoned and orphan when her father dies. After marrying Alphonse Frankenstein, she plays the role of a self-sacrificing mother and thus dies while taking care of her adopted daughter. The innocent maid of the family, Justine, who is like a sister to the children of the house, is executed for being accused of William's murder. Elizabeth, Victor's love of life, is shown waiting for her love throughout the novel but when she marries him she is murdered by the monster on her wedding night. She does not get a chance to live the day which she had been dreaming her entire life. The female monster is aborted even before she could be animated.

Istvan Csicsery Ronay, Jr. gives seven beauties of a science fiction which shall be searched for in this text to see whether it fulfils the criteria or not. The first beauty of a science fiction according to Istvan Csicsery Ronay is the use of *fictive neology*, i.e. new words which are used to paint the unknown world being described in a text. In *Frankenstein,* the title itself seems to be a franken word since according to Oxford dictionary, the name Frankenstein is also used as an adjective to refer to somebody as a monster or as being monstrous. And it was after the publication of her novel that the titular word/name was added to the dictionary. Other than this, the present novel does not seem to contain explicit new words coined by the author. The reason behind this might be that Mary didn't have any formal education and studied on her own through books from her father's library. Another reason might be that the scientific developments were new to the age and so the author could not think of or didn't need to coin new words to write the story. But there are many words and phrases, the usage of which, seems to be new and rare to the readers of her age, like these examples from the text: "...satiate my ardent curiosity..." (2), "...to embark in a seafaring life..." (2), "I shunned the face of man; all sound of joy or complacency was torture to me; solitude was my only consolation—deep, dark, death like solitude" (77), "...eyes were now lighted up with indignation, now subdued to downcast sorrow, and quenched in infinite wretchedness" (200), "...the forms of the beloved dead flit before me, and I hasten to their arms..." (208), "The completion of my demoniacal design became an insatiable passion" (210), etc.

The second beauty Istvan talks of about science fictions is of the presence of a *fictive novum* which refers to the new things or concepts brought in by the author. The present novel efficiently employs this beauty; firstly, the title of the novel *Frankenstein, the Modern Prometheus* talks of Prometheus, the legendary character who brought fire to mankind and suffered greatly in return. But, Frankenstein is the modern Prometheus who tries to bring a spark to a collection of inanimate body parts due to which many innocent people lose their lives along with the culprit (Frankenstein) and humanity is exposed to danger. In a way, there is a new imaginative concept applied to borrowed legendary character of

Prometheus. Secondly, we can take the form of the story as a *novum*. The story begins with letters from a brother on a voyage, Walton, to his sister, Margaret. Within these letters Frankenstein verbally narrates his entire story to Walton which further includes the letters written to him by his family members, letters and signs by the monster, the speeches made by the monster, references to 'P.L.', 'Plutarch's Lives', 'Sorrows of Werter', etc. and the conversations of the Lacey family. In the scenario of the literary contributions of her age, such a presentation of a story was a *novum*. Lastly, the basic idea of the tale is itself a *novum*; amidst the world of scientific technologies and the developments, a student of physical sciences and chemistry, aspires to create spark in inanimate body parts but ultimately creates a monster and faces the consequences.

Future History is the next beauty of science fiction according to Istvan who says that the readers of Science Fiction expect to see something which is connected to their present but at the same time is not yet realized. Frankenstein wants to create a human being and hence, makes use of scientific processes like galvanism, electrolysis, etc. to bring dead matter into life. And now this has actually happened in reality in the modern world. We have successfully created a life in the form of a sheep known as 'Dolly'. Scientists at Synthetic Genomics, California, have also been successful with their experiments to create artificial life nicknamed 'Synthia'. Therefore, the novel has proved itself to be a specimen of science fiction and the writer seems to be far ahead of her age.

While reading the main part of the novel, we find the associations of science and technology becoming more prominent. We come across the names of some scientists like Cornelius Agrippa, Albertus Magnus, and Paracelsus; terms like Natural Philosophy, electricity, potassium, mathematics, psychology, anatomy, etc. We find that various scientific theories are used extensively to enable Victor succeed in "bestowing animation upon lifeless matter" (Shelley 38). The known scientific laws are misused or violated by the character according to the story. But the author deliberately allows this to happen only to give a dramatic touch. She does not do so in order to criticise the scientific concepts but just to create an atmosphere suitable to the context. Istvan addresses this feature as the fifth beauty of science fiction known as *Imaginary Science* according to which the authors violate the currently known scientific laws to project the imaginary future through literature.

Istvan says that a science fiction contains *Science-fictional Sublime* of "literary space-time". As such, there are no space-time concepts in the novel in compliance with age. But the world in which Frankenstein dreams of being famous is, no doubt, obsessed with scientific developments and advancements taking place all around his world, as well as in the nineteenth century. Moreover, the age was deeply influenced by Darwin's theory of *Origin of Species* and this is what is noticeable in the author's thoughts as well as the titular hero's ambition to create a being. The very well-known concept of *Science-fictional Grotesque* (concepts which seem to be oxymoronic according to the present common sense) stands next in the list of the beauties of a science fiction. The same is true of the novel *Frankenstein.* Victor had been nurturing the ambition of becoming God-like by creating a living human being through the powers of science and technology. But the result made it clear that however powerful science becomes, it will still be absolutely impossible. Therefore, this notion of a man aspiring to become God seems to be absurd but at the same time spectacularly interesting.

Finally Istvan says that a good science fiction also contains a *Parable*. Light and fire seem to have been used as symbols to indicate towards the carefulness required while using them. Light kills darkness and fire gives warmth but too much light makes us blind and being too close to fire burns us. The same is the case with science and its principles, their use within the limits is beneficial, but, beyond limits, they can prove to be dangerous and fatal. We also find incidents when humanity is shown more important than selfish goals. Frankenstein refuses to create a female counterpart for the monster with the thought that the monster family shall destroy the whole humanity and world. He takes this decision in spite of being aware that the monster shall destroy his entire family in fury of the refusal of his demands. He also stakes his own life and meets a painful death while pursuing the monster to kill it, in order to save the rest of the world from the bearing the consequences of his 'creativity'. Therefore, we find *parable* too in the story of the novel.

So we find that all these points act as real beauty spots of the fascinating story of Frankenstein and his creation, along with helping in the analysis of the novel.

We find a similarity between the situation of the monster and that of Adam. Adam is said to be the first man according to Christian concepts and Frankenstein is not only the first being created by a human but also the first 'human' being of its kind due to his disproportionate, giant and grotesque stature. He also refers to himself as Adam while he is in conversation with his creator:

> But *Paradise Lost* excited different and far deeper emotions.... I often referred the several situations, as their similarity struck me, to my own. Like Adam, I was apparently united by no link to any other being in existence; but his state was far different from mine.... He had come forth from the hands of God a perfect creature, happy and prosperous, guarded by the especial care of his Creator; he was allowed to converse with and acquire knowledge from beings of a superior nature, but I was wretched, helpless, and alone. (Shelley, 118)

He relates himself to Adam for they share the situation of being the lonely first creation of their individual kinds. At the same time, he is intellectual enough to recognise that Adam's case was better than his because God loved His creation in all aspects and also created Eve for him as a companion. But in the monster's case, he was created by Victor as a grotesque, hideous, giant being and was detested, shunned and isolated by him. Moreover, when he asked for a female companion for himself, Victor refused (though for rational reasons). But all these realisations filled the monster with hatred towards his creator and towards the entire humanity and made clear by Shelley: "Many times I considered Satan as the fitter emblem of my condition... (118), "'Hateful day when I received life!'... 'Accursed creator!.... Satan had his companions, fellow devils, to admire and encourage him, but I am solitary and abhorred'" (119). "No Eve soothed my sorrows nor shared my thoughts; I was alone" (120).

The novel involves frequent use of double inverted commas, dashes, hyphens, commas, exclamatory mark, question mark, semicolons and colons. The novel also makes use of various text forms like letters, notes, journals, inscriptions, books, etc. Written in an epistolary form, the novel begins with letters from Robert Walton to his sister Mrs. Saville, in which he shares his experiences during the journey about the sea expedition. The letters are numbered as Letter 1, Letter 2, Letter 3 and Letter 4 and each letter gives specific details about the place and date on which it was written. But Shelley just mentions the century in which the letters were written but not any specific year. Probably, she knew well-in-advance that the message of her story shall be relevant in all ages. To look at Letter 1 for instance, it specifies the details of the addressee 'To Mrs. Saville, England' and mentions the place and date

'St. Petersburgh, Dec. 11th, 17—'. Letter 2 was written on 'March 28th, 17—' from Archangel. Letter 3 was written on 'July 7th, 17—' and Letter 4 on 'August 5th, 17—'. The body of these letters contains elaborated description of the geography, climate, season, directions, distance and landscape of his surroundings as noticeable in the lines: "I am already far north of London...Petersburgh...a cold northern breeze play upon my cheeks..." (1), "...the floating sheets of ice...dangers of the region...a very high latitude; but it is the height of summer..." (8), etc.

All these letters frame the background of the story and it is the fourth letter which continues till the end and narrates the complete story within twenty-four chapters. The paragraphs are sometimes very short and sometimes long. Some exclamatory sentences and swearing expressions seem to be used to give emphasis. For example, "Great God!" (122), "CURSED, CURSED creator!" (125), "The God of Heaven forgive me!" (73), "D—n the fellow!" (55), etc. Therefore, when based on a scientific idea, written in an age of scientific advancements and aiming at the uses and abuses of science, the novel automatically acquires the feature of science in its language. Also, being a science fiction, it makes use of scientific English, the language of the register of science. So we shall now look for the seven features given by Halliday which contribute to the difficulties in the scientific English of *Frankenstein.*

Taking up the first feature of Scientific English, i.e. *interlocking definitions*, Mary Shelley wrote this novel by just making some modifications in her dream. It is completely a story written by an unprofessional writer for an ordinary reader. So we do not find any such 'interlocking definitions'. But yes, we do find the structures and contexts complex due to the use of poetic expressions, complex sentence structure, multiple subordinate clauses in a sentence, "spontaneous overflow of powerful feelings" and long sentences. For instance:

> But when I discovered that he, the author at once of my existence and of its unspeakable torments, dared to hope for happiness, that while he accumulated wretchedness and despair upon me he sought his own enjoyment in feelings and passions from the indulgence of which I was forever barred, then impotent envy and bitter indignation filled me with an insatiable thirst for vengeance. (Shelley 210)

In such expressions, a reader is expected to be attentive to understand what is being said. There are so many subordinate clauses and phrases attached with the main sentence that at times simple meaning also seems to be complex or distorted. It becomes difficult sometimes to remember who is the speaker and to whom, about whom or about what is the speaker talking.

Next, Halliday says that scientific English consists of *Technical Taxonomies* (cluster of words highly packed in concepts). We do not find such technical taxonomies in the grammatical structures of the story because as already stated the story talks more about the aesthetic, spiritual, emotional and humanistic prospects than scientific and technical. It is explicitly literary and implicitly scientific. Somewhere in the middle of the story, scientific and technological concepts gain weight but they remain only in the background. That is why slight indications of technical taxonomies are noticeable only in those chapters of the novel where Frankenstein begins his studies about creating a life and till he actually creates a monster. In these chapters, we find concepts about science and its various fields and experimentation. Some of the instances of such technical taxonomies are:

> A mind of moderate capacity which closely pursues one's study must infallibly arrive at great proficiency in that study; and I who continually sought the attainment of one object of pursuit and solely wrapped up in this, improved so rapidly that at the end of two years, I made some discoveries in the improvement of some chemical instrument which procured me great esteem and administration at the university. (Shelley 37)

> I paused, examining and analyzing all the minutiae of causation, as exemplified in the change from life to death, and death to life, until from the midst of this darkness a sudden light broke in upon me—a light so brilliant and wondrous, yet so simple, that while I became dizzy with the immensity if the prospect which it illustrated, I was surprised that among so many men of genius who had directed that inquiries towards the same science, that alone should be reversed to discover so astonishing a secret. (Shelley 38)

We also find taxonomy of highly ordered construction of the form of the novel. The story within story structure seems to be a little complex for an ordinary reader at one attempt. In between the story's narration by Frankenstein to Walton, about the past of the former, we are brought to their present conversation on the ship. This flash-on and flash-back technique increases the complexities of the text's structure.

Special expressions (sentences stretched very long) are also found in the novel but they are not according to their definition as given by Halliday. They are according to the emotional and philosophical orientation of the story. The speakers express their feelings through such special expressions which make the language a little difficult to be comprehended. For example,

> Its productions and features...the phenomena of the heavenly bodies undoubtedly are in those undiscovered solitudes.... I may there discover the wondrous power which attracts the needle; and may regulate a thousand celestial observations, that require only this voyage their seeming eccentricities consistent for ever...to induce me to commence this laborious voyage with the joy a child feels when he embarks in a little boat...on an expedition of discovery up his native river. (Shelley 1-2)

> ...I was occupied by exploded systems, mingling, like an unadept, a thousand contradictory theories and floundering desperately in a very slough of multifarious knowledge, guided by an ardent imagination and childish reasoning, till an accident again changed the current of my ideas. (Shelley 26)

The next feature of science fiction is quite prominent in the novel. Be it emotional outburst or some information related to science, we find many examples of *Lexical Density* every now and then in the story. Particular lexical words are used according to the context in the novel and their manner of distribution in the grammatical structure increases the level of difficulty in the comprehension of the text. Some of the instances of the same are:

> I am practically industrious—painstaking, a workman to execute with perseverance and labour—but beside this there is a love for...the marvelous intertwined in all my projects, which hurries me out of the common pathways of men, even to the wild sea and unvisited regions I am about to explore. (Shelley 7)

> I never saw a more interesting creature: his eyes have generally an expression of wildness, and even madness, but there are moments when, if anyone performs an act of kindness towards him or does him the most trifling service, his whole countenance is lighted up as it were with the beam of benevolence and sweetheart that I never saw equaled. (Shelley 11)

As noticed above, too many lexical items in a sentence lead to *Syntactic Ambiguity* because of the stretching of a nominal clause to a great extent or due to the conversion of clauses into nouns. This is the next feature of scientific English of this novel. Sometimes a single sentence contains many clauses and sometimes the ambiguity increases because too many ideas are given in a single sentence with the help of punctuation marks like comma, semicolon, hyphen, inverted commas, etc. Given below are some examples of the same:

> I have seen…the most beautiful scenes of my own country…visited the lakes of Lucerne and Uri, where the snowy mountains descend almost perpendicularly to the water, casting black and impenetrable shades, which would cause a gloomy and mournful appearance where it not for the most verdant islands that relieve the eye by their gay appearance…lake agitated by a tempest, when the wind tore up whirlwinds of water and gave you an idea of what the water spout must be on the great ocean…waves dash with fury the base of the mountain…an avalanche and where their dying voices are still said to be heard amid the pauses of the nightly wind…the mountains of La Valais, and the Pays de Vaud; but this country, Victor, pleases me more than all those wonders. (Shelley 144)

> The abrupt sides of vast mountains…me; the icy wall…glacier overhung me; a few shattered…around; and the solemn silence… presence—chamber of imperial nature…brawling waves…vast fragment, the thunder…cracking, reverberated…mountains, of the accumulated ice, which…immutable laws, was ever…and torn, as if…their hands. (Shelley 83)

> In the meanwhile…herbage, and the green…flowers, sweet…eyes, stars of…woods; the sun became warmer, the nights clear and balmy; and my nocturnal…me, although…of the sun, for…daylight, fearful… which I entered. (Shelley 106)

We also find instances of *grammatical metaphor* in the novel, i.e. nominal verbs, verbal nouns, i.e. substitution of one grammatical class by another. The speakers make use of nominal forms of verbs and adjectival forms of nouns. For example,

> You have probably waited impatiently for a letter to fix the date of your return to us…. (Shelley 58)

> Absence cannot have rendered you callous to our joys and grief, and how shall I inflict pain on my long-absent son? (Shelley 58)

> Why do you call to my remembrance? (Shelley 88)

Finally due to all the above-mentioned features of the language of *Frankenstein* we find some semantic gaps *or semantic* discontinuity. This means that scientific English expects from the readers to follow its semantic leaps in order to a conclusion. For example in chapter IV, we find that Frankenstein is studying the sciences and is toiling for his aim of creating a being of life but then suddenly chapter V begins:

> It was in dreary night of November that I beheld the accomplishment of my toils…collected the instruments of life infuse a spark of being into the lifeless thing that lay at my feet…by the glimmer of the half-extinguished light, I saw the dull yellow eye of the creature open, it breathed hard, and a convulsive motion agitated its limbs. (Shelley 43)

Here no direct statement says that he has created the being by following such and such steps in a sequence. The readers are expected to understand that he has succeeded in creating a life but it is in the form of a monster and not a normal human being. When Frankenstein narrates his story to Walton, we do not find any specific punctuation marks or any other indication of when he is directly talking to Walton, at present, on the ship and when is he narrating his past to Walton in direct speech. Here the readers again are presumed to be attentive and intelligent enough to understand the story told at present as well in the flashback.

Therefore, the language of the novel satisfies in its own way, all the essential features of scientific English given by Halliday.

Now, analyzing the novel from the point of view of the narratological devices given by Dino as discussed in the first chapter, we find that the author has beautifully used the flashback and flash-forward techniques. Frankenstein makes use of *analepsis*, i.e. he goes back to his past. The monster also recalls all his experiences when he meets Frankenstein in the latter's story. So here we again find an instance of analepsis. We also find incidents of *prolepsis* in the text, for example, Frankenstein tells Walton that after listening to his story the latter shall quit from his adventurous undertaking or journey towards North Pole; and the story ends with Walton's letter stating his return from his journey.

The life of Frankenstein, his experiences and his story form the *diegesis* of this novel because it is the main plot. The monster's story about his own experiences since the time of his 'creation' and the story of Felix and Safie form the *metadiegesis* or *hypodiegesis* because these come within the story of Frankenstein. *Extradiegesis* is formed by Walton's letters which include the main story.

The actual chronological events of this narrative form its *story*. These chronological events are Frankenstein's entire story, monster's creation, monster's experiences, monster destroying the whole family of Frankenstein, Frankenstein following monster in a vow to kill it, Walton and his giving shelter to dying Frankenstein on their ship and listening to his story, Frankenstein's death, monster finally disappearing forever. This is the actual story of the novel or *fabula* in terms of Tomashovsky. The way the story is presented, i.e. the frame narration of the story forms the *sjuzhet* or *discourse*.

The novel involves *first-person narration* because Walton is an observer and listener to the story of the main character. He is an *embedded* or *active listener* of Frankenstein's story. Due to this, Walton becomes the *focalizer* because we are confronted with the main story through his *subjective perception* of Frankenstein or his *subjective narration* of the tale. And thus the setting of the frame story is Captain Walton's ship in the Arctic Ocean surrounded by ice on all sides. But the incidents of the main story cover the entire Europe especially the University of Ingolstadt, Geneva, the great mountain range called Alps, France, England and Scotland. Therefore, Frankenstein and his story become the *focalized objects* because they are described and reproduced by Walton in his letters.

The novel uses the device of *frame narrative* as Walton's letters contain Frankenstein's story which further contains monster's story. In each frame, we find a different narrator. We also come across *hermeneutics* and *proairetic* codes in the novel. Coming across Walton's letters to his sister, Margaret, we are anxious to know whether he will succeed in his expedition through the sea or not. When Frankenstein creates a monster in stead of a human being, a question arises in the readers' minds—what will happen next? These are all examples of hermeneutics codes because they raise questions for some time on the part of the readers. *Proairetic codes* are also present in the novel, for example, when the monster expects some love, sympathy and friendship from the people he confronts and helps, especially the Lacey's, we already have an idea that because of his ugly features, abnormal physique and detestable countenance, he shall receive hatred from everyone.

Conclusion

Shelley has used the extensive knowledge of the most recent scientific developments of her day to analyse as well as criticise the more dangerous implications of the scientific method and its practical results. She contrasts the science working upon the detailed and reverent descriptions of nature with the hubristic manipulations of the elemental forces of nature to serve man's private ends. Her use of science in the book directly relates to the many discoveries of the seventeenth, eighteenth and nineteenth centuries, specifically the discovery made by Benjamin Franklin about the scientific properties of electricity.

Scientists like Erasmus Darwin, Humphry Davy and William Nicholson frequented the house of Shelley. The diary entries written around the time of *Frankenstein* say that she was gathering scientific background for the novel by reading Davy's *Elements of Chemical Philosophy*. Thus, she was influenced by his discovery of the process of electrolysis. Victor is also shown to be influenced by famous scientists like Paracelsus, Albertus Magnus and Erasmus Darwin. The novel relates to the scientific discovery made by Luigi Galvani, the most. Luigi discovered that bioelectric forces exist within living tissues. This discovery known as Galvanism is a science of healing and rekindling life via electric current.

The novel is thus grounded in scientific research, predicts what might be possible in future, given new scientific discoveries and offers a humanistic critique of either specific technological inventions or the very nature of scientific thinking. But it also warns the readers against the dangers of crossing the limits while advancing in scientific developments. Victor uses the theories of many great scientists, as already enumerated before, in the process of infusing life into dead matter. For this purpose, he collects the different parts from different bodies lying in graves. He does not give any forethought to the results of the experiment he is going to do for the first time in history. He does not calculate the resultant proportion of ugliness and gigantic stature in the creature he is going to bring to life by supplying electric current through the selected huge body parts.

Victor has the power and he recognises it but does not utilise it in a thoughtful manner. In spite of having all the control and the knowledge in the beginning, he renders himself powerless and pitiable in the hands of his own creation. This is what Shelley wants to focus upon possibly. Science does not have the powers to turn somebody into God just by the magic wand. God has created this nature and has control over man and his birth and death. Man has given the term science to the detailed and experimental study of these natural elements and to the creation of artificial aids for his own benefits and comforts. So, man does not have the right to even compare his substitute power with the original one of God. Science is somewhere required to enable us to live a civilised life better than the primitives and animals. But thoughtless application of scientific knowledge to attain selfish interests ultimately makes our presence more meagre and pitiable. The lust for more power makes us all the more weak and dependent for existence and sustenance. Victor is excited to become the first person in the world who has the power to bring 'spark' in dead matter. But in pursuing this aim, he gradually loses his peace, his happiness, his family, his wife and his health struggling for survival. Therefore, what Shelley expects from her readers to learn is that scientific discoveries and advances must be pursued only if they do not have negative effects on our lives. Now, let's see whether this novel fulfils other conditions of being a good science fiction.

Therefore, we can say that *Frankenstein* is certainly the first Science fiction along with being a Gothic tale. It satisfies all the conditions of being categorised as a science fiction; it possesses Istvan's seven beauties of a science fiction and Halliday's seven features of scientific English, though up to a limited extent. It is a narrative which employs the required narrative devices appropriately to mix them properly with the scientific and literary elements brought together. Falling into the category of a Soft SF, it employs such themes which makes it an evolutionary type of science fiction belonging to the early nineteenth century.

REFERENCES

Coffin, Caroline, Ann Hewings and Kieran O' Halloran ed. "Some Grammatical Problems in Scientific English" by M.A.K. Halliday. *Applying English Grammar.* London: Hodder Headline Group, 2011.

Csicsery-Ronay, Istvan Jr. *Seven Beauties of Science Fiction.* Middletown: Wesleyan UP. 2008.

Felluga, Dino. "General Introduction to Narratology". *Introductory Guide to Critical Theory.* January 31, 2011. Purdue U. January 18, 2014.

Mundra, J.N. *Advanced Literary Essays.* Bareilly: Raza Barqui Press, 2002.

Shelley, Mary. *Frankenstein.* New Delhi: Peacock, 2009.

'Prometheus'. *Theoi Greek Mythology (Exploring Mythology in Classical Literature and Art).* Aaron J. Atsma, New Zealand. 29 May 2014.

❑❑❑

Mrs Dalloway: Culmination in the Cult of Experimentation

MANI MEITEI

JACOB'S Room is Virginia Woolf's first full-fledged "new" novel. It illustrates the advantages she evidently enjoyed in her experiment with the new technique after having mastered the craft within the limits of a short story. Surely with *Jacob's Room*, Virginia Woolf's break with the tradition of Wells, Bennett and Galsworthy is complete, and with it she finds conveniently a rank among James Joyce, Dorothy Richardson and Marcel Proust. The agility with which she started the novel continued till 1927 the year *To the Lighthouse* was published. *Mrs Dalloway* and *To the Lighthouse* belong to a serious creative period of Virginia Woolf, and they have earned her a permanent place as one of the architects of the modern stream-of-consciousness fiction. These two novels are marked by the growing maturity of Virginia Woolf in controlling and displaying the newly gained literary vision rather than showing a literary urgency that inspired *Jacob's Room.* A diary entry, dated June 23, 1922 shows her planning to write *Mrs Dalloway*: "I shall produce *Mrs Dalloway in Bond Street* as the finished product.... Now what will they say about Jacob! Mad, I suppose: a disconnected rhapsody; I don't know" (*WD* 53).

Unlike as in *Jacob's Room* Virginia Woolf could evolve a proper novelistic vision in *Mrs Dalloway*. Inspired by *Ulysses*, she could well know what she was going to do in *Mrs Dalloway*. This time her reactions to Joyce became genuine, that her difference from him became much more interesting than the similarities, such that people often wrongly call *Mrs Dalloway* a parody of *Ulysses.* Compared with Joyce's egocentricity in *Ulysses Mrs Dalloway* is plainer, less confusing, less enigmatic and less of a literary jargon in the use of literary methods. Strictly speaking, *Mrs Dalloway* is by far the greatest of all Virginia Woolf's novels from the experimental point of view, with a new focus on the innovation of a vision and design; and correspondingly this innovation operates simultaneously on the levels of philosophy and style. The recognition that the values of the moments in human life are governed by the flux of all time units of past, present and future has led to the inconsistency and losing of the exactitude of character delineation in favour of a dynamism of human beings under the scrutiny of an omniscient mind. Characterization is not, therefore, based on the interaction between plot and character's action but on the inner telepathy of the characters. The shortcomings in characterization in *Jacob's Room* are taken care of as Virginia Woolf is guided by a vision to make "her characters indulge in the easy telepathy of those who cohabit in the same brain" (Albright 1-2). To make life more meaningful, time is to be kept in a continuum, in the way things occur in mind's consciousness: a confluence of past, present and future. In *Mrs Dalloway* characters dive in this stream of time, and thereby they appear not static personalities but personalities related to the fluidity and dynamic process of subjective time, *la durée*. Therefore, *Mrs Dalloway* is not complete if seen from the angle of a single time perspective. The limitation of this being consciously felt, Virginia Woolf renders the mind of her character(s) as a conglomeration of all times—past, present and future—in terms of memories, the moment itself, fantasies and simultaneous perceptions.

This different mode of narrative requires a different type of plot in the novel, not based on what is going on in the external world as actions and events but on mental reactions of characters to a certain situation. Since the novelist captures mind's movement in time, a linear method of narrative is not applicable to the new novel. Yet, significantly some plot pattern can surely be carved out in *Mrs Dalloway*. The vision is clear in the form of the theme that centres round "life and death, sanity and insanity…to criticize the social system, and to show it at work, at its most intense" (*WD* 63). The framework of *Mrs Dalloway*, as given below, would make the starting point of a closer analysis.

Mrs Dalloway, a woman in her fifties, married to a stolid M.P. and mother of a gangling seventeen year old girl, goes out shopping in preparation of an elaborate dinner party that evening which will be attended by the Prime Minister. She ruminates as she goes about. The fine June morning takes her mind delightfully to the romantic past over twenty years at Bourton, then she herself a girl of eighteen. Again the chance meeting with the Whitbreads on the Westminster Street links up the present with the past. A number of undying names of places and persons come up with renewed feelings: her love affair with Peter at

Bourton (now back from India), again his thought brings her a sense of warm nostalgia, her relationship with Sally Seton and her marriage with Richard. Simultaneously, an interesting and independent plot runs on a different plane, to present and contrast "the world seen by the sane and the insane side by side" (58). Septimus Warren Smith, a veteran of war, aged about thirty, is suffering from nervous disorders, as a result of shell-shock and the haunting memory of his friend Evans who was killed just before the Armstice. He contemplates suicide and is treated by a psychiatrist called Sir William Bradshaw, who is threateningly on him. Unable to tolerate the brutal human nature and its imposition on him he commits suicide on this day, and the news of his eventual death by suicide as reported by Bradshaw saddens Clarissa in the midst of her party, and she feels a sudden sense of identification and communion with the man she has never known.

This is all what can be said about the novel externally. But above all, what happens below the primary conscious level is the most important thing in a stream-of-consciousness novel. The merging of all personalities into one consciousness without the presence of the individuals and at the same time the drawing in of the reader from one consciousness to another are the new ways of looking at characterization; and this has been superbly achieved in *Mrs Dalloway*. This suggests Virginia Woolf's concept that personality is always in a state of flux. Besides this, in the interior monologues of her characters she shows that time is also constantly swinging backward and forward, all signifying beyond a shade of doubt the concept of dualism. It is worth seeing how Clarissa's mind is dramatized by Virginia Woolf who all the time guides the character's mental meanderings in her role of "selective omniscience" in Normal Friedman's terms, which "differs from ordinary omniscience…in that the author shows what is going on rather than telling us about it" (Naramore 95). One knows Virginia Woolf is interested in the presentation of momentary impressions of the characters with vivid photographic reality. Here is the kaleidoscopic mind of Clarissa, as she walks down the Westminster streets on the morning of a June day to buy flowers. Her mind records whatever comes, memories, fantasies, images that meet and merge by a free association of ideas. The following excerpt from the book will illustrate the basic mental functioning of the heroine, Clarissa at a moment:

Mrs Dalloway said she would buy the flowers herself.

For Lucy had her work cut out for her.... And then, thought Clarissa Dalloway, what a morning—fresh as if issued to children on a beach.

> What a lark'. What a plunge! For so it had always seemed to her when, with a little squeak of the hinges, which she could hear now, she had burst open the French windows and plunged at Bourton into the open air. How fresh, how calm, stiller than this of course, the air was in the early morning; like the flap of a wave; the kiss of a wave; chill and sharp and yet (for a girl of eighteen as she then was) solemn, feeling as she did, standing there at the open window, that something awful was about to happen; looking at the flowers, at the trees with the smoke winding off them and the rooks rising, falling; standing and looking until Peter Walsh said, 'musing among the vegetables?—was that it?—'I prefer men to cauliflowers'—was that it? He must have said it at breakfast one morning when she had gone out on to the terrace—Peter Walsh. He would be back from India one of these days, June or July, she forgot which, for his letters were awfully dull; it was his sayings one remembered; his eyes, his pocket-knife, his smile, his grumpiness and, when millions of things had utterly vanished—how strange it was!—a few sayings like this about cabbages. (5-6)

This is typical of the stream-of-consciousness method employed by Virginia Woolf. In it a number of the experimental techniques—flash-black, montage, durational flux, free association of ideas, memories, fantasies and a variety of moods—are present, and again what is reflected all through is Clarissa Dalloway's spiritual self in her indirect interior monologue. The narrative looks like an unreeling film, in which ideas blend themselves—some are recreated, recaptured by similitude in moods as compared with the present moments, exclusively, with little conscious or intellectual effort whatever. In order to call up the past Clarissa's mind withdraws itself from the present very often, but this association is unique and serves the purpose of the stream-of-consciousness fiction.

It is noticed how the scenes and mental situations work up together in Clarissa's mind in about twenty pages in the beginning of the novel. Her mind as she walks along the streets of Westminster to buy flowers recollects her affair with Peter at Bourton twenty years ago when she was eighteen. Once the idea of Peter comes it allows her mind to remain in fantasy for he is coming back from India one of these days. Then her mind is pregnant with related images that help gather Peter's impression, "his eyes, his pocket-knife, his smile, his grumpiness." A shift in the thought occurs. Now she remembers the last night's talk at the embassy about the war being over. Further down the Park she meets Hugh Whitbread, whose appearance steals her again in the past Bourton life, digging up her quarrel with Peter and her choice of Richard, etc. Suddenly she is concerned about the whereabouts of Richard at present parenthetically. The thought runs alongside the past life of Clarissa. Then she comes to a halt in front of a shop from which she had bought gloves before the war as she remembers. Greeted by Miss Pym she stands before the florist shop, and is startled by the pistol shot like sound of a royal car. She speculates about who the dignitary is. In this way Clarissa's consciousness permeates through time indivisibly. And a number of characters are also derived from her consciousness. Both of these methods of conveying character consciousness and character depiction, one must admit, are suggestive of the basic concepts of the subject matter of the stream-of-consciousness novel.

In more or less the same way, the past life at Bourton is rendered in the consciousness of Peter, Sally Seton, Hugh and Richard Dalloway. The same details as dramatized in Clarissa's interior monologue are flooded with subjective reflections, evoking in turn different reactions depending on the personal sense of experience. Bourton exists in Clarissa's mind as a source of happiness in contrast to the uncertainties of the post-war period of London, while at the same time it is the "death of the soul" to Peter Walsh, who was rejected by Clarissa at Bourton in favour of Richard in due course. In Regent's Park Peter snores after which his mind goes back to Bourton:

> He sat down beside her, and couldn't speak. Everything seemed to race past him; he just sat there, eating. And then half-way through dinner he made himself look across at Clarissa for the first time. She was talking to a young man on her right. He had a sudden revelation. 'She will marry that man,' he said to himself. He didn't even know his name.
>
> For, of course, it was that afternoon, that very afternoon, that Dalloway had come over; and Clarissa called him 'Wickham'; that was the beginning of it all. Somebody had brought him over; and Clarissa got his name wrong. She introduced him to everybody as Wickham. At last he said 'My name is Dalloway!'—that was his first view of Richard—a fair young man, rather awkward, sitting on a

desk-chair and blurting out 'My name is Dalloway!' Sally got hold of it; always after that she called him 'My name is Dalloway!' (68-69)

To Peter the past is not as happy a phenomenon as it is to Clarissa Dalloway. But in his involuntary memory of the past also Virginia Woolf symbolically represents the mechanism of automatic thinking in the subconscious mind of a character in the stream-of-consciousness novel. However, apart from its stream-of-consciousness function the interior monologue of Peter has done a magnificent piece of character delineation. It is that the more his indirect interior monologue continues with its backward and forward movements the more of Clarissa Dalloway's character in the past is revealed. Charles Hoffman has this to say:

> …Peter's most obvious function is to disclose Clarissa's past. He becomes the primary tool Virginia Woolf employs in her "tunneling process," the means utilized to "dig out beautiful cave behind my characters," to "tell the past by instruments, as I have need of it." As he remembers his and Clarissa's past throughout the novel, Peter reveals facts about life which the other characters never discuss, providing the reader with an external view of his history. (Carlson 58)

True, it is through Peter's reactions and feelings that the reader is able to build Clarissa's character up. In his annoyance she is "timid; hard; arrogant; prudish" (66) and again his failure to marry her is due to her "coldness" and "woodenness" (68). And in his admiration for her she is a symbol of "courage," "social instinct" and above all she is a "perfect hostess" (69). If this is true the same is true of Peter in Clarissa's mind for "They went in and out of each other's minds without any effort" (70).

As regards Sally Seton's reaction to Bourton it is marked by impassioned feelings of joys and pain: "She never had a penny to her name in those days, and going to Bourton always meant some frightful pinch. But going to Bourton had meant so much to her—had kept her sane, she believed, so unhappy had she been at home" (208). Admittedly, this kind of evoking different reactions of different characters to the same thing is one of the most effective methods of representing Virginia Woolf's vision of reality in her experimental novels.

In *Mrs Dalloway* Virginia Woolf analyses two worlds—one represented by the sane and the other by the insane in the characters of Clarissa and Septimus respectively. They are represented in the novel as being separate and different worlds opposing each other, but at a deeper level they are part and parcel of one and the same mind. Notably, it is as much a book of abnormal psychology as is considered civilized. Despite the unusual calmness of the period in which *Mrs Dalloway* and *To the Lighthouse* were written such as to call them products of "emotions recollected in tranquillity," the former is not devoid of the symptoms of her life—of both insanity and sanity. In *Beginning Again* what Leonard Woolf says may be recalled: "...in her life the symptoms would not go and she passed across the border which divides what we call insanity from sanity" (76). In Septimus Virginia Woolf also presents one of the worst symptoms of the First World War that is "shell shock" (a term coined for the first time by a Cambridge psychologist and army medical officer, Charles Mayers in 1915) or "war neurosis" as is also known. It is, as James D. Page says, "a psychological strain of forced and continued exposure to the terrifying and dangerous sounds and scenes of battle that precipitated symptoms" (142-43). Septimus's mental derangement continues even after the war, being a chronic case, and his obsessive fear of sound is evident when he hears Edgar J. Watkiss say "'The Prime Minister's Kyar'," with the sudden coming of the royal car in Bond Street. To Septimus "The world has raised its whip; where will it descend?" (17) is the reaction. His fear increases "as if some horror had come almost to the surface and was about to burst into flames" (18). Even the sounds of music and a motor horn are ghastly to him. His background as well as the momentary impressions of his is necessary for understanding and investigating the root cause of his abnormal behaviour. Septimus was one of the first to volunteer, and had served with great distinction; won promotion; and was married to Lucrezia, an Italian girl, without loving her and unable to have a child, rejoined his earlier post of a clerk, lost interest in literature and had nervous mental break-down. He saw women burnt alive, watched indifferently shells explode, saw his friend Evans killed, and saw the cruelty of human nature: "that human beings have neither kindness, nor faith, nor charity beyond what serves to increase the pleasure of the moment. They hunt in packs. Their packs scour the desert and vanish screaming into the wilderness" (99).

The world he has represented in the novel is from the angle of the war and destruction, the collapse of human values—the great War and its effects, brought upon the shore of human civilization. Being disturbed by the horror of the War he experienced he has lost mental balance and becomes a victim of the evils of the whole social system. Being very sensitive, and unable to separate himself from own War experience he drifts into, being again vulnerable to the shadow of the nether world of death, giving himself up to unconsciously incoherent speeches, emotional outburst, self-confusions. His is a case of psychogenic amnesia, caused by the sight of his friend Evans, killed in the War, and his exposure to the terrifying circumstances. Trapped in the ever worsening psychotic problems, he nourishes a death wish, baffling and frightening his wife, and starts living in a world of his own by withdrawing from the activities of the world. He complains that he sees visions, Evans, death, faces; he hears voices calling his name; he talks to himself and to a dead man and speaks about absent things. In one sense haunted by hallucinations his mind is distracted to non-existent things, sounds, odours, feels non-existent stimuli as if in a dream and to the extent of being bizarre. Rezia's agony as reflected in her soliloquy shows the gravity of Septimus's insanity, caused by fear, neurotic paranoia, meditating on self-destruction:

> Everyone has friends who were killed in the War. Everyone gives up something when they marry. She had given up her home. She had come to live here, in this awful city. But Septimus let himself think about horrible things, as she could too, if she tried. He had grown stranger and stranger. He said people were talking behind the bedroom walls…. He saw things too—he had seen an old woman's head in the middle of a fern…. Suddenly he said, 'Now we will kill ourselves,'…and she felt he was going from her and she caught him by the arm. But going home he was perfectly quiet—perfectly reasonable. He would argue with her about killing themselves; and explain how wicked people were; how he could see them making up lies as they passed in the street. He knew all their thoughts, he said; he knew everything. He knew meaning of the world, he said. (74)

His direct and prolonged exposure to violence during the War makes him keep rapport with the unseen, unknown, all a post-War symptom of hallucination and schizophrenia. With such a man, had he enjoyed sex and married life he would have certainly evaded the tragic end. To make things worse, the doctors who treat him are of no avail. Dr. Holmes who asks Rezia to make Septimus "notice real things, go to a music hall, play cricket" (29) and take up some hobby in an effort to give temporary relief from the traumatic memory by making him interested in things outside himself is on him and is "the repulsive brute, with the blood-red nostrils" (102). Sir William Bradshaw, the psychiatrist, too insists on his taking rest in bed so that proportion be restored. And in order to restore balance he says if proportion fails he has to take the support of police and good society which would take care that "these unsocial impulses, bred more than anything by the lack of good blood, were held in control" (113). Resorting to brutishness and sending to the asylum as suggested by the doctor will only aggravate the Septimus's condition. Another method of treating Septimus is "Conversion," which is in the form of war and is blood thirsty. This total lack of human consideration will have inevitable tragic consequences. Through the creation of these two doctors Virginia Woolf attacks the "cynicism about doctors from their lack of comprehension of her own altered states and frightening sensations during her illnesses" (Thomson, www.jstor.org/stable/10.1525/jung). Septimus is tired and the only way to escape from this trauma is death by suicide for "through Septimus, Virginia Woolf is able to describe both death and the brink of insanity where it is difficult to know what is really there, and the deep depression which the sufferer believes is only to be resolved by suicide" (*ibid.*). In Septimus's life and death Virginia Woolf has criticized the social system: the evils of war as a triumph of civilization as Peter reflects when the ambulance runs with the dead man and the dry impositions of the doctors like policemen and branding of the neurotic as unsocial or anti-social elements. The Septimus case history is a real reproduction of Virginia's own bouts of insanity that attacked her five times.[1]

The inclusion of Septimus portion in *Mrs Dalloway* is of great significance in a stream-of-consciousness novel because it symbolizes the duality of the human mind. Without this point taken into consideration the Septimus part would be like drawing a red herring across the trail like "the Man of the Hill" portion in *Tom Jones*, liable to do some damage to the structure of the novel. But the intention of the novelist for representing the consciousness of the insane as against that of the sane is to achieve a convincing reality through syllogism. The Septimus portion, although, running independently in the book without even a recognizable link with the Clarissa part, has satisfactorily accomplished the duality of human personality, this time not in one person but in two persons, each representing one of the two cerebral hemispheres of the brain. This view is in conformity with both the Oriental and the Western thoughts, philosophic, mystical and scientific. Appraising the scientific division of brain into two cerebral hemispheres by A.L. Wigan, a nineteenth century British physician in his book *The Duality of the Mind* Paul Bakan concludes thus:

> "...it takes one hemisphere to have a mind"; and since the brain has two hemispheres it is normal to have two minds. In fact, Wigan argued "the two hemispheres of the brain are really...two distinct and entire organs...each as complete...and as fully perfect...for the purposes it is intended to perform, as are the two eyes." Wigan also concludes that each cerebrum (i.e., hemisphere) is a whole organ of thought; that two thought processes can occur simultaneously, one in each cerebrum; that each cerebrum is capable of a separate volition, often opposing that of the other cerebrum; that the incoherence of insane consciousness results from an alternating intermixture of two trains of thought; and that the superiority of a disciplined scholar lies in his power of habitually combining the attention of both brains to the same object. (Pope and Singer 160-61)

If carefully examined the two minds of Clarissa and Septimus would appear to have been interwoven so as to form one personality, one brain—half sanity, half insanity. Originally, Virginia Woolf intended to make Clarissa die herself at the end of the party but the plan was dropped as she created Septimus to die. Septimus is Clarissa's "double," a Dostoevskian term. And it is in his death, the news of which is given by Sir William Bradshaw towards the end of Clarissa's party that "plunges her nevertheless into a deep fantasy and identification with the unknown man who is now dead" (Edel 131) and whom she did not meet and who by no means is outside her social life. Thus, Dr. Bradshaw is the thread which links Clarissa Dalloway to Septimus and his death. In order to substantiate this point how the subtle communication or intermixture of the two takes place a discussion at length is necessary.

The two realities are not poles apart but are the "opposite sides of the same coin" (Lehmann 51). Virginia Woolf says about him: "here is a young man who carries in him the greatest message in the world, and is moreover, the happiest man in the world, and the most miserable" (93). These two contrary states of the human mind, happiness and misery, reveal the worlds of Clarissa and Septimus respectively. Once more when Clarissa feels "it was very, very dangerous to live even one day" Septimus practically kills himself on a day when he also feels that it is very difficult to live even one day. His death by throwing himself from a window has a close symbolic relation with Clarissa's throwing a "shilling to the serpentine" that appears twice in the book. "Fear no more the heat of the sun," Clarissa's motif is repeated by

Septimus when he says "Fear no more, says the heart in the body; fear no more" (154). Furthermore, they have striking similarities in physical appearance. Clarissa's "ridiculous little face, beaked like a bird's" (13) reminds one of Septimus's "pale-faced, beak-nosed" (17). Of other revealing aspects both Clarissa and Septimus bear, communication is one. Septimus suffers from want of communication of a "new religion and the cult of universal love" because human beings are corrupted by inability to comprehend things inside the soul. In Septimus's hatred of this there lies the deep irony of life manifested by Virginia Woolf: her protest against the masculine domination, the cruellest form of which is war. So beneath Septimus's suffering lies the greatest shock of the age. On the other hand, Clarissa's is universal love and even her hatred of a particular character or individual is reduced to her hatred of the idea represented by the individual and *not* the individual. This shows how her hatred of Miss Kilman is converted into a hatred of ideas. Therefore the essential difference between Septimus and Clarissa is the former's "inability to isolate and oppose the objects of his hatred" and he "cannot dissociate, as Clarissa and the narrator can, monstrous ideas from the people who personify them" (DiBattista 45). For him everything is mixed up, indifferent and hateful, and the ultimate communication he has is through his death: "Death was defiance. Death was an attempt to communicate, people feeling the impossibility of reaching the centre, which mystically, evaded them…" (204).

Towards the end of *Mrs Dalloway* the grim world of Septimus overshadows the gay world of Clarissa, and it is here that the two streams of life meet. Clarissa's experience or perception is inseparable from the fate of Septimus, whose death brings her extremes of sorrow:

> Always her body went through it, when she was told, first, suddenly, of an accident; her dress flamed, her body burnt. He had thrown himself from a window. Up had flashed the ground; through him, blundering, bruising, went the rusty spikes. There he lay with a thud, thud, thud in his brain, and then a suffocation of blackness. So she saw it. (203)

Now the real link between the Clarissa and the Septimus parts or the Septimus part and the rest of the novel is established not through a logical plot pattern but through a closely-knit psychological and symbolic relation. The feasibility of combining these two otherwise disparate movements on the logical and rational ground is one of the greatest and most admirable achievements in the whole stream-of-consciousness fiction. The basic emphasis in the stream-of-conscious novel that personalities are one and the same thing in all probability according to the new psychological discoveries and hypotheses is not only a realization but certitude in the modern experience. And Virginia Woolf's claim to it sounds more authentic for the reason that her own life given to close examination reads like the dual life of Clarissa and Septimus. Throughout her life she lived under the shadow of recurring madness, and through the creation of Septimus, her alter ego, she tried to fend herself off the recurring fit of insanity, but in vain, Septimus shook her very fountain of life. In the late thirties, she became miserable for she was not able to communicate reality, which was in turn eclipsed by the horror of another great war approaching. This is evidently shown in *Between the Acts*, in which she took up a pageant as her raw material of fiction, escaping from a reality—War—she was quite long acquainted with, unable to communicate what she wanted to, as the object itself could not be isolated from hatred itself. Life became more and more unbearable for her; it was a 'walking shadow', 'a tale told by an idiot'. She knew insanity started touching at her bone; she became sick, a symptom of serious nervous breakdown from which recovery would be difficult or impossible. In order to escape from this dreadful disease she threw herself in the river Ouse and took her life. Therefore, Septimus's insanity and death and Clarissa's sanity in *Mrs Dalloway* were the meaningful release of the artist's sickness, prophesying her ultimate fate. If Clarissa Dalloway is Mrs. Woolf herself in *Mrs Dalloway* then "Indeed Septimus can be seen as the negative parallel of Clarissa Dalloway, who herself steers clear of the threatening gulf of madness only at the price of repressing her passions and desires, becoming a cold but brilliant woman highly admired in patriarchal society" (Moi 12). Virginia Woolf was not only a visionary artist but also a prophetic writer like Shelley. The novel is a many-dimensional novel bearing the visions of her creator. Phyllis Rose comments thus:

> Creativity and madness are the central subject of this book: the impulse towards life and the impulse towards death, the sane and the insane, representing two impulses or currents within Virginia Woolf.... Mrs Dalloway represents Woolf's fullest self-portrait as an artist; it contemplates the relationship between her own madness and her creativity. (126)

In *Mrs Dalloway* the three persons, Clarissa Dalloway, Septimus and Mrs. Woolf are subsumed as one entity, already much has been said about Clarissa and Septimus. When the shadow of the Second World War started looming large both the Woolfs decided to end their lives in the event of an invasion by the Nazis, and Mrs. Woolf was at the breaking point and thus took her life by drowning in the river Ouse on 28 March 1941. In her suicide note she wrote: "I have a feeling I shall go mad. I cannot go on longer in these terrible times. I hear voices and cannot concentrate on my work. I have fought against it but cannot fight any longer. I owe all my happiness to you but cannot go on and spoil your life" (http://creativecommons.org), re-echoing Septimus.

Yet, it is significant to note that in *Mrs Dalloway* Virginia Woolf does not appear to be satisfied with the presentation of the abstract nature of life or reality. Keeping this as a point of primary importance she goes on applying some devices, like the chiming of Big Ben, a motor car and an airplane, vitally merged with the whole structure. Their function in the novel is one of achieving unity and tightening the seemingly formless mental reality. For instance, the chiming of Big Ben from the beginning of the novel to the end incessantly imposes a pattern on the timelessness of the flow of characters' psyche, strictly engulfing the whole fleeting history of the characters into a recognizable diurnal setting. By virtue of its counter-movement against time-montage the actual time taken in narrating the day's happening is convincingly put in about sixteen hours. Each sound of the clock serves like a division of the book. The striking of the clock divides the book into many parts or chapters. Thus it compensates, above all, for the absence of conventional chapter divisions in *Mrs Dalloway,* and the time sequence sets the plot development. The following is the way in which time falls: 10-11 a.m. Clarissa's shopping in London; the appearance of the motor car and the skywriting airplane; Septimus and his wife Rezia are seen in Regent's Park. 11 a.m.: Clarissa at home; Peter visits Clarissa. 11.30 a.m.: Peter leaves Clarissa's for Regent's Park; Septimus in Regent's Park hallucinating; Peter takes notice of Septimus, and he recollects Bourton. 12 noon: Septimus enters Bradshaw's clinic in Harley Street; Clarissa lays down her green dress. 1.30 p.m.: Septimus goes out of Bradshaw's clinic; lunch is served to Richard Dalloway and Hugh Whitbread at Lady Bruton's in Brook Street. 3 p.m.: Richard comes home. 3.30 p.m. Clarissa's mind distracted by her anger with Miss Kilman; Miss Kilman at tea and at church; Elizabeth's bus ride. 6 p.m.: Septimus commits suicide; party at Clarissa's. 3 a.m.: Clarissa is lost in the thought of death.

If one knows this function of Big Ben and if one follows this movement the reading of *Mrs Dalloway* will be a happy experience. However, the avoidance of formal divisions and the weaving together of the time units inside of the structure of the novel achieve the maximum effect of breadthwise and depthwise narrative. Yet, on a closer scrutiny it would appear that despite its success as a mechanical device to measure consciousness from time to time, major characters like Clarissa and Septimus revolt against it. Clarissa gets obviously annoyed when it strikes three resounding blows. She is "so annoyed, at her writing-table; worried; annoyed" and her room is flooded with the sound of "its melancholy wave" (130) because her mind transcends all limits of time and space. Harvena Richter argues that the use of Big Ben is "to contrast the emotional quality of their durée," referring to the duration of Clarissa and Septimus. Septimus too tries to free himself from the imposition of clock time by attaching to his "ode to Time,' an immortal ode to Time" (78). Commenting on Septimus's defiance of clock time Shiv K. Kumar writes:

> He lives in a perpetual communion with the past through his recollections of his deceased friend Evans. Even his ultimate suicide seems to symbolize his complete defiance of the tyranny of clock time as represented by Sir William Bradshaw, who has taken upon himself the task of restoring the mental balance of his patients. (75-76)

Thus, Big Ben's function in *Mrs Dalloway* is very important and it signifies the stream-of-consciousness method of the novel. First, it shows that anything outward or mechanical is temporal and as nimble as a delusion against the all-pervading flux of experience. Second, its systematic recurrence occupies the place of plot in a plotless novel-form. Third, each chiming of Big Ben makes the interior monologue change from character to character, suggesting that every moment something new takes place in human consciousness. This is so because the will of the mind in terms of thoughts impinges in time and "that impingement is symbolized by the striking of the clock" (Daiches 207).

So far in the stream-of-consciousness novel the novelist's concern to show that consciousness is independent and one man's consciousness works differently from that of another is explicit, and the attempt towards it is successful. The novelist is, however, not satisfied with it alone, for he wants to show that under certain circumstances various characters respond almost equally to certain objects or situations in such a way that individual factors or private mental egocentricities get blended to make a multiple focus, submerging all private mental differences. The novelist, then, employs space montage to get that effect of collective consciousness. In *Mrs Dalloway* Virginia Woolf's use of a motor car and an airplane works in that direction. The motor car with blinds drawn in front of Mulbery's shop, at a point of time, draws the attention of Edgar J. Watkiss, Clarissa, Septimus, boys, passers-by and old ladies on the top of omnibuses. Down St. James's Street in Buckingham Palace it again catches the attention of a small crowd in which Sarah Bletchley, Emile Coates and Mr. Bowley are included. The psychic activities of these characters at this moment are being fixed on the object moving while confining their consciousness to a static time. Similarly a skywriting airplane keeps the whole consciousness of London fixed upon one object in space for a time. Mrs. Coates, Mrs. Bletchley and Mr. Bowley see the airplane skywriting from a different angle and in Regent's Park by Septimus and Rezia from another angle. It flies over Greenwich, St. Paul's and over London like a "bright spark; an aspiration; a concentration; a symbol (…) of man's soul" (32). And Clarissa at her Westminster home asks her maid who opens the door "What are they looking at?" (33).

In this way, the function of the motor car and the skywriting airplane is to unify the diverse and chaotic movements of different human minds. This is the fundamental artistic function in a stream-of-consciousness novel to control the movement of character consciousness by methods other than one. Therefore, the motor car and the airplane do fulfill one of the basic functions as to how the irrational mind is to be kept under artistic control. Jean O. Love views thus:

> The airplane and the motor car are similar in their function, the plane supplanting the car and repeating the physical events associated with it. Like the car, the plane is an agent of unity and a nodus of transcendent consciousness. When it appears overhead, the airplane becomes at once the focus of consciousness that had agglomerated around the mysterious automobile. (152)

Keeping in view the nature and vision of reality Virginia Woolf wants to portray in her novels a further inquiry would reveal a lot more. Herself absorbed in the peculiar vision of reality, Virginia Woolf is not ready to paint the car and the airplane at their face value, nor is she interested in the description of objective reality, as soulless as it is. Rather she mystifies the objective reality to the extent of ambiguity. No one can give the identity of the royal dignitary inside the car for sure; all speculations revolve round the Prime Minister, the Queen and the Prince of Wales. The same is the case with what is written by the advertising plane. All the letters are vague—purposely vague. This lack of objective detail is to support her own subjective vision of life and to evoke curiosity in the reader. This curiosity once more substitutes for the traditional narrative's "what happens next?" Had she not mystified these two objects she would seem to define states of reality on material basis, which would make the book awkwardly insensitive to the demands of the stream-of-consciousness novel.

In *Mrs Dalloway* Virginia Woolf seems to have done maximum justice to her conviction as a stream-of-consciousness novelist. It is, however, common knowledge by now that she has been charged with a failure to portray three dimensional, convincing or memorable characters. Charges like this have come from responsible and respectable quarters of criticism. Yet, it should not be hard to see that such charges suffer from an inability to distinguish two basically different trends like comparing metaphysical poetry with Augustan poetry. Parallel judgment of two distinctly different modes of narrative may not be a viable proposition in literary criticism. In an age when reason became deceptive, and reality became far removed from being static and when the difference between fact and fantasy became obscure or at least marginal what novelistic formula or standard of judgment remained without undergoing a drastic change? True literary judgment should be based on the work itself or what it is, and not on what it ought to be or should have been under altered circumstances.

Clarissa Dalloway, Septimus, Peter, Rezia are the most adorable portraits of Virginia Woolf, whose vision of reality in terms of essence is fulfilled by them. With a new ethic of personality—the semi transparent mystical vision—put forward she tries to paint her characters as a model of Mrs. Brown. And these characters who can become equal to Mrs. Brown are also major characters, and those who fail to come up to that level are minor characters. Therefore one should not be disturbed by puerile comments like the one given here by Arnold Bennett:

> As regards character-drawing, Mrs Woolf (in my opinion) told us ten thousand things about Mrs Dalloway, but did not show us Mrs Dalloway. I got from the novel no coherent picture of Mrs Dalloway. Nor could I see much trace of construction, or do ordered movement towards a climax, in either *Jacob's Room* or *Mrs Dalloway*. Further, I thought that both books seriously lacked validity.
>
> .... The people in them do not sufficiently live, and hence they cannot claim our sympathy or even our hatred: they leave us indifferent. (Majumdar and Allen 190)

The minimum one may fairly reasonably submit here (with due deference to Arnold Bennett is that if someone fails to see Mrs. Dalloway, one is definitely to thank oneself for that. Mrs. Dalloway is very much there, figuring in a rich way, not only in the length and breadth of the novel but also at the depth of the novel. She is not only clearly visible; she is impressive and readers, who are not unduly allergic to a new technique of characterization, find her worth. In that, she is very much with Clarissa and Emma and Tess.

In reading Virginia Woolf's stream-of-consciousness novels one must be acquainted with the new way in which she looks at character. She is not ready to give comedy and tragedy thereby to arouse the reader's sympathy for or hatred of the characters for there is no such a thing as bring emotion to the character painting. There is a distance between the reader and the character, but the novelist is able in a stream-of-consciousness novel to bring the two together by means of interior monologue. One knows that the reader is drawn inside the mind of the character directly or indirectly in such a novel. She is meticulous in character delineation: seldom can a traditional novelist give such a full view of a character in so short a passage from *Mrs Dalloway*:

> Peter Walsh! All three, Lady Bruton, Hugh Whitbread, and Richard Dalloway, remembered the same thing—how passionately Peter had been in love; been rejected; gone to India, come a cropper; made a mess of things; and Richard Dalloway had a very great liking for the dear old fellow too. Milly Brush saw that; saw a depth in the brown of his eyes; saw him hesitate; consider; which interested her, as Mrs Dalloway always interested her, for what was he thinking, she wondered, about Peter Walsh? (118)

One finds how the bits of information by way of recollected impressions or reactions build up Peter's character. It is the reader's task to gather such bits to have a full personality of characters in *Mrs Dalloway*. This is also true of other stream-of-consciousness novels of Virginia Woolf. In like manner Clarissa Dalloway's character is also done with admirable success through a number of interior monologues of various characters including her own. She is the central character in the novel: a woman of fifty two, a mother of one girl, Elizabeth, and wife of a middle ranking M.P. She has all human virtues and a few weaknesses. She is a perfect hostess and has all love and sympathy to give and has none to hate except that she hates ideas of flesh, selfishness, suppression, hypocrisy and above all war. Highly perceptive and sensitive to the extreme that she knows "people almost by instinct" (11) and resides almost in the past as much as in the present. She "had a narrow pick-stick figure; a ridiculous little face, beaked like a bird's" and "had nice hands and feet; and dress well" and "had the oddest sense of being herself invisible; unseen; unknown" (13) very shrewd and "a far better judge of character than Sally" and "purely feminine" (84) a "queer fish" (86) in an atmosphere of different people of different tastes; "enjoyed life immensely" (87) and basically a "snob" (134). Of other qualities she has, she is an admirer of Sally Seton, a strong trait of lesbianism in her, holds scissors, mends clothes with a needle and has a social instinct comfortably. The examination shows that Clarissa is a strong, convincing and valid character and she has nearly perfected the vision of her creator. She is, in J.K. Johnstone's words "convincing, because she has about her the reality, the infinite divinity, and beneath diversity, the essential unity of life" (Johnstone 339).

As in any other novel the characters in *Mrs Dalloway* fall into two categories: major and minor. The division is based on the ability to occupy a continuity in the minds of other characters and on how they weave the various character consciousness to unify the novel's structure, and lastly on the symbolic representation of the novelist's vision of reality. Clarissa Dalloway, Septimus, Rezia and Peter Walsh are strongly framed characters who can leave deep and lasting impressions on the minds of the readers, and they are the major characters who frequently live in their past, and form a basic unity of the structure of the novel with the help of the past in an unconventional way. Clustered around them are a number of characters faintly drawn like Richard Dalloway, Sally Seton, the Whitbreads, Elizabeth, Lady Bruton, Doris Kilman, Dr. Holmes and Sir William Bradshaw. Of these characters except the last two, others pivot round the concentric circle of Clarissa and Peter. As for the last two, the orbital move they have is around the Smiths.

The success of *Mrs Dalloway* depends much on the four major characters whose past background has enormously enlivened the eventful June day. It may doubtlessly be concluded that without their past background the book's strength will be under-rated and the characters "would be mere pasteboard figures lacking in depth were they not portrayed against a background of their earlier selves" (Newton 35). Surely, this dependence on the past background marks the structure of the novel, a fact which will stand out more clearly at a later stage, when an attempt is made to compare *Mrs Dalloway* with another Virginia Woolf masterpiece, *To the Lighthouse*.

From these and other points of view *Mrs Dalloway* is undoubtedly a serious experimental novel. The book in itself the high watermark of the symbolic use of language with accompanied impressionistic images, parentheses, ellipses, prepositional participles, co-ordinative conjunctions, rhetorical devices and among others the psychological awareness of sex and gesture in determining the consciousness of characters. To render some illustrations:

1. Impressionistic use of images (to suggest the insane world of Septimus)

   She brought him his papers, the things he had written, thing she had written for him. She tumbled them out to the sofa. They looked at them together. Diagrams, designs, little men and women brandishing sticks for arms, with wings—were they?—on their back; circles traced round shillings and sixpences—the suns and stars; zigzagging precipices with mountaineers ascending roped together, exactly like knives and forks; sea pieces with little faces laughing out of what might perhaps be waves: the map of the world. Burn them! He cried. Now for his writings; how the dead sing behind rhododendron bushes; odes to Time; conversations with Shakespeare; Evans, Evans, Evans—his messages from the dead; do not cut down trees; tell the Prime Minister. Universal love: the meaning of the world. Burn them! He cried. (163)

2. Parentheses (indicating a shift in the character's thought or the author's comment)

Against such moments (with women too) there contrasted (as she laid her hat down) the bed and Baron Marbot and the candle half-burnt. (37)

Sinking her voice...Lady Bradshaw (poor goose—one didn't dislike her) murmured how, 'just as we were starting, my husband was called up on the telephone, a very sad case. A young man (that is what Sir William is telling Mr Dalloway) had killed himself. He had been in the army.' (203)

3. Ellipses (to indicate the non-verbal flow of different ideas)

   There was no time to let Mrs Williams know, and really Rezia thought it very, very annoying, when she caught sight of the hat and thought...perhaps...she...might just make a little.... Her voice died out in contented melody. (161)

4. Prepositional participles

   Rezia, sitting at the table twisting a hat in her hands, watched him. (155)

   Gliding across Piccadilly, the car turned down St James's Street. (21)

5. Co-ordinative conjunctions (to indicate uninterrupted thought)

   And Lucy stopped at the drawing-room door, holding the cushion, and said, very shyly, turning a little pink couldn't she help to mend that dress?

   But, said Mrs Dalloway, she had enough on her hands already, quite enough of her own to do without that. (44)

6. Anaphora

   The ladies were going upstairs already, said Lucy; the ladies were going up, one by one, Mrs Dalloway walking last.... (183)

7. Anacoluthon

   Now the door opened, and in came—for a single second she could not remember what he was called! So surprised she was to see him.... (45)

8. Synesthesia

   First a warning, musical; then the hour, irrevocable. The leaden circles dissolved in the air. (6)

9. Free association of ideas and sensory images

> 'What are they looking at?' said Clarissa Dalloway to the maid who opened the door.
>
> The hall of the house was cool as a vault. Mrs. Dalloway raised her hand to her eyes, and, as the maid shut the door to, and she heard the swish of Lucy's skirts, she felt like a nun who has left the world and feels fold round her the familiar vials and the response to old devotions. The cook whistled in the kitchen. She heard the click of the typewriter. It was her life, and bending her head over the hall table, she bowed beneath the influence, felt blessed and purified, saying to herself, as she took the pad with the telephone message on it, how moments like this are buds on the tree of life, flowers of darkness they are, she thought (as if some lovely rose had blossomed for her eyes only); not for a moment did she believe in God; but all the more, she thought, taking up the pad, must one repay in daily life to servants, yes, to dogs and canaries, above all to Richard her husband, who was the foundation of it—of the gay sounds, of the green lights, of the cook even whistling, for Mrs. Walker was Irish and whistled all day long—one must pay back from this secret the pad, while Lucy stood by her, trying to explain how. (33-34)

In this passage Virginia Woolf uses a number of sensory feelings, tactile, auditory, kinesthetic, and visual, suggesting and revealing Clarissa's immediate experience trailing through a variety of images. All the sensory feelings, every sound, every feeling of touch and sight as Eliot says, an "a direct sensuous apprehension of thought" and as in Donne, every immediate feeling in the sensibility of Clarissa Dalloway is her experience. Out of the fusion of these images, is composed a new structure, a unique kind of new meaning close to poetry. It is precisely in this rich, creative way that *Mrs Dalloway* emerges as a prime novel of considerable charm.

Further, one notes Virginia Woolf's attempt to make language not only a suitable medium to represent the fluidity of human personality or of reality but also as flexible as possible to resemble the complex state of what is to be communicated. They are symbols through which is rendered what is evanescent and short-lived, and thus one gets rid of whatever is commonplace and ordinary in the linguistic phenomenon.

Mrs Dalloway is a threshold of the genre of the stream-of-consciousness fiction in English literature and it is a crusade of the modern experimental fiction against the tradition of fiction that is not of the age. The book stands out as a testimony to the radical ways in which modernism in British fiction was defined and expressed in the most complex and sophisticated manner, all to show modern sensibility. No student of the subtleties of this new technique can ignore this rich response which renders the twenties of the twentieth century a highly creative and experimental phase in the perspective of modern fiction. That it did not continue for long and later novelists chose to return to the traditional partially or completely indicates not so much of the inherent inadequacies of the new technique as the onrush of new pressures, new impositions on the novelists' minds including the most momentous imposition, the invasion of politics in the Thirties and Forties and of diverse aspects of class-consciousness later. By all means Modernism still remains an inseparable project of the Postmodern thinking for they share many common tenets.

NOTE

1. Virginia Woolf's biographer Hermione Lee writes in *Madeness*, the tenth section of her book *Virginia Woolf* (1996) published by Vintage Books, New York: "Five times in her life (four of them bet the ages of thirteen and thirty-three) she suffered from major onslaughts of the illness and in almost all (possibly all) of these attacks she attempted to kill herself," 171.

WORKS CITED

Albright, Daniel. *Personality and Impersonality: Lawrence, Woolf and Mann.* Chicago: Cambridge University Press, 1978.

Bakan, Paul. "Two Streams of Consciousness." *The Stream of Consciousness: Scientific Investigations into the Flow of Human Experience*. Eds. Kenneth S. Pope and Jerome L. Singer. New York: Planum Press, 1978.

Bennett, Arnold. "Another Criticism of the New School." *Virginia Woolf: The Critical Heritage*. Eds. Robin Majumdar and Allen McLaurin. London: Routledge and Kegan Paul, 1975.

Carlson, Julia. "The Solitary Traveller in *Mrs Dalloway*." *Virginia Woolf: A Collection of Criticism*. Ed. Thomas S.W. Lewis. New York: McGraw-Hill, 1975.

Daiches, David. *The Novel and the Modern World*. Chicago: The University of California Press, 1984.

DiBattista, Maria. *Virginia Woolf's Major Novels: The Fables of Anon.* New Haven: Yale University Press, 1980.

Edel, Leon. *The Psychological Novel 1900-1950.* Ludhiana: Lyall Book Depot, 1965.

http://www.creativecommons.org/licences/by-ndnc/1.0/fi/deed.en. Dated 8.6. 2014.

Johnstone, J.K. *The Bloomsbury Group.* London: Secker and Warburg, 1954.

Kumar, Shiv K. *Bergson and the Stream of Consciousness Novel.* New York: NYUP, 1963.

Lee, Hermione. *Virginia Woolf.* New York: Vintage Books, 1999.

Lehmann, John. *Virginia Woolf and Her World.* London: Thames and Hudson, 1976.

Love, Jean O. *Worlds in Consciousness: Mythopoetic Thought in the Novels of Virginia Woolf.* Berkeley: University of California Press, 1970.

Moi, Toril. 1985. *Sexual/Textual Politics: Feminist Literary Theory.* London: Routledge, 1995.

Naramore, James. *The World Without a Self: Virginia Woolf and the Novel.* New Haven: Yale University Press, 1973.

Newton, Deborah. *Virginia Woolf.* Calrton: Melbourne University Press, 1956,

Page, James D. *Abnormal Psychology.* New Delhi: Tata McGraw-Hill Press, 1985.

Rose, Phyllis. *Women of Letters: A Life of Virginia Woolf.* London: Routledge and Kegan Paul, 1978.

Thomson, Jean. "Virginia Woolf and the Case of Septimus Smith" *The San Francisco Jung Institute Library Journal*, Vol. 23, 3, August 2004, 55-71. URL: http://www.jstor.org/stable/10.1525/jung.1.2004.23.3.55.

Woolf, Leonard. *Beginning Again: An Autobiography of the Years 1911-1918.* London: The Hogarth Press, 1964.

Woolf, Virginia. *A Writer's Diary.* Bungay: Granada, 1981.

——. *Mrs Dalloway.* Penguin Books, 1974.

❑❑❑

T.S. Eliot and the New Criticism

ARINDAM MODAK

IT is not for nothing that T.S. Eliot is considered an immediate influence on the emergence of the New Criticism. The objective approach to literature that was to be espoused so ardently by the New Critics has been given a strong voice to by T.S. Eliot. Ransom himself considered him "one of the most important sources of a *new* criticism" (Ransom, *New Criticism* 140, emphasis added). Besides being a critic, Eliot was also a poet and a religionist. His criticism was conservative, marked by his scholarship, finesse, and a distinctive prose style. But his poetry, both in tone and structure, broke new ground. Again, in terms of religion he was an Anglo-Catholic. In this respect, he famously declared in the introduction to *For Lancelot Andrewes* in 1928 that he was a Royalist in politics, an Anglo-Catholic in religion, and a Classicist in literature (Ransom, *New Criticism* 137). Each aspect of his personality invigorated the others, but Eliot never allowed one aspect to come in the way of the others. Eliot's critical taste, as he himself confessed, was that of a Classicist. He termed poetry "autotelic" (Eliot, *Function* 23), and believed that judgement of poetry should not be vitiated by religious, moral, political, and social considerations. In Eliot's later years, religious, political, and philosophical writings formed the bulk of his prose literature, and there was little literary criticism as such; but his earlier views remained unchanged.

Eliot found English criticism in a state of disorder and sought to impose order on it. For him, art was a quest for order in life, and criticism, in turn, was a quest for order in art. But the English critics were not in a position to voice clearly their differences, not to speak of composing those differences among themselves. The difference, Eliot discovered, originated from the contending claims of Classicism and Romanticism. England, a country of individual liberty, has always upheld the claims of Romanticism. So Classicism, which demands allegiance to an outside authority, has never had a sound footing in England. But, for Eliot, the matter is not a question of national or racial prejudice, but one of rightness; and Eliot ironed out the problem by arguing in favour of Classicism. He argues that showing allegiance to an outside authority is quite natural in a human being, whether he is showing it as a citizen to the government of his country or as a believer to the church. Similarly, in criticism also there should be some common criterion of judgement to which the critic has to submit. But the champions of individual liberty rely upon, what Eliot, quoting Middleton Murry, calls in *The Function of Criticism*, their 'Inner Voice' (Eliot, *Function* 23). This being their sole guide in the interpretation of a work of art, there is no external standard to vindicate such interpretation. So, instead of facts, which alone can bring out the reality about a work of art, the critic gives his own opinion about it. The result is that fact is supplanted by fiction. The function of criticism, which Eliot holds in the eponymous essay to be "the elucidation of works of art and the correction of taste" (23), thereby gets defeated. In order to fulfil this function of fact-finding, Eliot implores the critic to be objective in his approach. He prescribes two things to attain this objectivity. Primarily, his "highly developed sense of fact" (31) will prevent the intrusion of his personal opinion into his judgement; and secondly, his tools of "comparison and analysis" (32) will help him understand the position of the literary work in terms of its modification by and of other literary works, and bring out its ontological significance. For example, Eliot takes up the popular judgement on Swinburne that the beauty of Swinburne's verse is the sound, and he had little visual imagination, and remarks that such inference can be made only through the comparative method. He compares lines and passages from Swinburne with those of other poets, and makes the observation how, unlike in other poets, in Swinburne there is no complete realisation of the musical or imagistic or ideational value of a word; in other words, Swinburne does not correlate a word with its objective content. Thus, Eliot puts in practice Arnold's 'touchstone' method. But unlike Arnold, he does not confine himself to the same lines and passages. He chooses lines similar to the ones under discussion. And here lies the importance of Eliot's insistence on the awareness of tradition. One can apply the comparative method of judging poetry only with a comprehensive knowledge of one's tradition.

Eliot had a strong sense of history. He is, however, not just a historical scholar who acquires knowledge of history, and relates this knowledge to the poet's life, or the intellectual propensity of his age, or the poetic school to which the poet belongs. Eliot is a historical critic who uses his knowledge of history for the literary understanding of the poet. He tries to understand whether a poetic tradition is in accord with the standard or norm set by the main stream or tradition of English or European poetry, as the case may be. Such historical knowledge does not usually determine the aesthetic value (whether a poem is good or bad) of literature. But Eliot goes beyond, and uses his historical learning as the basis for passing critical remarks. Here one may pertinently recall what he writes in "Religion and Literature" (1956): "The greatness of literature cannot be determined solely by literary standards; though we must remember that whether it is literature or not can be determined only by literary standards" (388).

One of Eliot's famous pronouncements about criticism is, "Criticism, by definition, is *about* something other than itself" (30). The concept of autotelic criticism is virtually non-existent. So the claim of interpretation as a valid tool of criticism is ruled out. In interpreting a work of art, the critic, instead of saying anything about it, gives voice to his own opinion. Similar is the case with Impressionism. It is a record of the impressions of a sensitive mind when it comes in contact with a work of art. Hence, it does not conform to Eliot's concept of criticism as faithful elucidation. Eliot also dismisses criticism that judges a work of art by its conformity to the precepts of the ancient critics; for such criticism does not enquire into the nature of a work of art sufficiently. To Eliot, the concept of true criticism is synonymous with the concept of scientific enquiry into the nature of an art-work. It is for this reason that Eliot considers Aristotle to be the ideal critic. Like a botanist or zoologist, Aristotle dissected a work to such an extent as to know about the underlying principle that could explain it. Other kinds of criticism are merely wish-fulfilment on the part of the critics. It is, again, this observation that led Eliot to believe that creative artists are more dependable as critics than professional critics, with the sole exception of Aristotle. Moreover, the creative labour expended in composing a literary work is critical in nature, involving "the labour of sifting, combining, constructing, expunging, correcting, testing" (30).

However, it is Eliot's theory of impersonality as propounded in his essay, "Tradition and the Individual Talent," written as early as 1919, that makes him the closest forebear of the New Critics. There he famously says, "No poet, no artist of any art has his complete meaning alone. His significance, his appreciation is the appreciation of his relation to the dead poets and artists" (15). Eliot conceives of 'tradition' as being built by the additions of newly created works to the existing ones. When a new work is created conforming to the standard traditional practice, the existing order is modified to accommodate the new creation; and subsequently, the proportionate relation of each work to the whole order is re-defined. But how is such a thing to be accomplished? Eliot asks the poet to adopt the process of what he calls "depersonalization": "The progress of an artist is a continual self-sacrifice, a continual extinction of personality" (17). The poet's mind acts as a catalytic agent that helps the poetic ingredients to mix in the consciousness of the poet, without itself taking part in the process. Eliot identifies the elements that go into the making of poetry as emotions and feelings. But the emotion perceived in art is quite different from the emotion as experienced in real life. The emotion of practical life gets transmuted in art to aesthetic emotion in the process of imitation. Thus an aesthetic distance is created. Moreover, the emotion in real life is too dominating to allow us to experience objectively the feelings in the heterogeneous and particular details of an experience. In the course of poetic transformation, through a process of gestation, emotion loses its intensity and is purged of any personal element. For obvious reasons, Eliot refutes Longinus's principle of 'sublimity' which subsists on the greatness or intensity of emotions. So Eliot's conclusion is: "Impressions and experiences which are important for the man may take no place in the poetry, and those which become important in the poetry may play quite a negligible part in the man, the personality" (20). The upshot of the whole issue, according to Eliot, is that "honest criticism and sensitive appreciation is directed not upon the poet but upon the poetry" (17).

Corollary to Eliot's theory of impersonality are his conceptions of the "objective correlative" and the "dissociation of sensibility," the first of which occurs in the essay, "Hamlet and His Problems," and the latter in "The Metaphysical Poets." The concept of the "objective correlative" is necessitated by the fact that the poet cannot transmit the emotions directly to the reader. He has to convey them through something concrete—"a set of objects, a situation, a chain of events," according to Eliot (145). His idea of the "objective correlative" is further clarified in the essay, "The Metaphysical Poets" where Eliot says that the Metaphysical poets "were, at best, engaged in the task of trying to find the verbal equivalent for states of mind and feeling" (289). The emotion the poet has to convey will be objectified through these, and as soon as these are presented to the reader, the particular emotion will be immediately evoked. The "dissociation of sensibility" is a characteristic fault of English poetry after the seventeenth century, which resulted from the bifurcation of thought and feeling. The antidote for this fault lies in the "unification of sensibility." For the composition of good poetry, ideas are not enough. The poet has to convert his thoughts or ideas into feelings, so that those feelings can steal their way into the reader's heart. Eliot cites the poetry of Chapman and Donne as possessing unified sensibility, while Tennyson and Browning, though they had ideas, could not "feel their thought as immediately as the odour of a rose." On the other hand, "A thought to Donne was an experience; it modified his sensibility" (287).

T.S. Eliot's critical principles left their indelible marks on the New Critical techniques. This has been acknowledged in unambiguous terms by John Crowe Ransom himself in the essay, "The Cathartic Principle": "I suppose our modern critics have learned to talk more closely about poems than their predecessors ever did. The closeness of Mr. Eliot in discussing a text may well be greater than anybody's before him, and he in turn may now be even exceeded in closeness by Mr. Blackmur, and perhaps others. These are close critics, and define our age as one of critical genius" (Ransom, *World's Body* 173). Eliot appears to Ransom to be "closer and more patient" than even Dryden and Dr. Johnson (Ransom, *New Criticism* 140), in his critical analysis. His critical writings have also "suppleness" and "charm" (139)—qualities which endow his writings with literary value.

Whatever affinities we may find between Eliot's critical pronouncements and the views of the New Critics, we must remember that in "The Frontiers of Criticism" (1956) he expressly disowns his affiliation to New Criticism. He writes: "I don't understand why the author should isolate me so sharply from the American critics; but on the other hand I fail to see any critical movement which can be said to derive from myself, though I hope that as an editor I gave the New Criticism, or some of it, encouragement and an exercise ground in *The Criterion*" (106). Much before that in 1935 itself he writes, "Literary criticism should be completed by criticism from a definite ethical and theological standpoint" (388). This shows that though Eliot started as a monistic critic, he gradually shifted to a pluralistic standpoint. But that hardly negates his influence upon the New Critics. It is clearly palpable in the basic tenets, especially objectivity and scientific evaluation of literature, that we associate with the New Criticism.

WORKS CITED

Borklund, Elmer. *Contemporary Literary Critics*. New York: St. Martin's Press, 1977.

Eliot, T.S. "The Function of Criticism." 1923. *Selected Essays*. London: Faber and Faber, 1961, 23-34.

——. "The Frontiers of Criticism." *On Poetry and Poets*. London: Faber and Faber, 1962, 103-18.

——. "Hamlet." 1919. *Selected Essays*. London: Faber and Faber, 1961, 141-46.

——. "The Metaphysical Poets." 1921. *Selected Essays*. London: Faber and Faber, 1961, 281-291.

——. "Religion and Literature." 1935. *Selected Essays*. London: Faber and Faber, 1961, 388-401.

——. "Tradition and the Individual Talent." 1919. *Selected Essays*. London: Faber and Faber, 1961, 13-22.

Prasad, B. *An Introduction to English Criticism*. New Delhi: Macmillan India Limited, 1965.

Ransom, John Crowe. *The New Criticism*. Norfolk, Connecticut: New Directions, 1941.

——. *The World's Body*. New York: Charles Scribner's Sons, 1938. Rpt. Baton Rouge: Louisiana State University Press, 1968.

Wellek, René. *A History of Modern Criticism, 1750-1950*. 8 vols. New Haven: Yale University Press, 1986.

Wimsatt, William K., Jr., and Cleanth Brooks. *Literary Criticism: A Short History*. New Delhi: Oxford and IBH Publishing Co. Pvt. Ltd., 1957.

❑❑❑

Transcreating Shakespeare in the Indian Cinema: A Retelling

SUNITA SINHA

> We were so sure...thought we always had our Indian audience.... The Indian audience would always love us and they did...they did... they always laughed at all the jokes. Cried at the right places...the most wonderful audience in the world.... They've changed...we've changed too.
>
> Mr. Buckingham in *Shakespeare Wallah*

"NEVER before has the western stage contemplated and manipulated the various cultures of the world to such a degree, but never before has it been at such a loss as to what to make of their inexhaustible babble, their explosive mix, the inextricable collage of their languages," remarked Patrice Pavis (Crossroads 1). Brian Singleton also reiterates, "Interculturalism and performance is perhaps the most talked about and controversial cultural practice of the late twentieth and early twenty-first centuries, characterized at best by a sharing and mutual borrowing of the manifestation of one theatre practice by another" (Singleton 628). In this scenario, "Shakespeare is an unusually prominent element of globalized theatre", remarked W.B. Worthen, "at once the vehicle of an international theatrical avant-garde..., of intercultural exchange..., of global tourism..., and of postcolonial critique" (Worthen). Enthroned enduringly in the domain of contemporary theatre, Shakespeare emerges as a powerful cultural token, whom Alan Sinfield compares to Jesus' garment, only touching the hem of which will cure the sick people. When Shakespeare is familiarized to the audience of other parts of the globe, the adaptations recurrently become cross-cultural reproductions and this demonstrates not only cross-cultural interpretations but also illumines the approaches from which Shakespeare is accepted by audiences in other cultures. The overwhelming number of theatrical outputs and academic criticisms on, non-Western Shakespeare at the turn of the millennium exhibits the central status of the so-called interculturalism in the field of Shakespeare and theatre.

"Every engagement with a Shakespearian text", writes Antony Tatlow, "is necessarily intercultural. The past really is another culture, its remoteness disguised by language that can occasionally appear as familiar as we seem to ourselves, whom we understand so imperfectly" (Tatlow 5). To translate a text is to disguise it anew, rendering it at once more familiar and more remote. As far as Shakespeare is concerned, either the translations produce familiarity by refurbishing the text's Elizabethan English to a modern rendition of the target language, so that non-Anglophone readers encounter the plays and poems as contemporary works or might be believed to hinder many of Shakespeare's 'bravura linguistic effects'. Kennedy's collection, *Foreign Shakespeare: Contemporary Performance* (1993) explores the circumstances and paradoxes of representing Shakespeare's plays in theatrical, critical, and cultural conditions substantially different from the traditions and tendencies of performance in the 'home countries', the major English-speaking nations (Kennedy, 1993, 2).

What happens when Shakespeare is performed without his language? In this context, Salman Rushdie makes a revealing observation as he says, "It is normally supposed that something always gets lost in translation. I cling obstinately to the notion that something can be gained." (Rushdie 16). However, despite Rushdie's proposal, not all commentators and spectators appreciate substantial Shakespearean amendments and believe that when Shakespeare's text is aggressively metamorphosed into a new language and a radically unfamiliar performative mode, something essential in Shakespeare disappears. To me, it appears that whatever be the linguistic losses that accompany translation, there have been significant gains in world of theatre and films. Though the conversion of the plays into contemporary English is not appreciated in English-speaking countries, but translation into contemporary dialogue achieves a much more direct audience understanding.

"Shakespeare was exported from the very beginnings of the Empire, when 'Hamlet and Richard II' were performed aboard the East India's good ship Dragon in the Indian Ocean from 1607 to 1610," remarked Professor Lawrence Gordon Manley, the Shakespeare expert. Shakespeare was introduced into Indian theatre more for projecting edification than for entertainment and was made available as an example of English culture and its superiority. Hence, Shakespeare became a tool for colonized nations seeking a voice. From India to Africa, "Shakespeare's works—especially 'The Tempest'—were used to talk back to the empire." One adaptation of "Othello" in mid-19th century Delhi made waves after a Bengali man was cast as the lead opposite an Englishwoman, an unprecedented role for an Indian.

In the early twentieth century, globalization seems to enable the "indigenization" and subversive appropriation of Shakespeare in postcolonial and developing nations. Moviemakers from non-Anglophone countries all over the world have resituated Shakespeare's plays in the idiom of their own language. Shakespeare has been treated as an icon of high culture, a "cultural trophy" (Rothwell 168) for centuries. The Bard stood tall as an insignia of Englishness that could be "used to legitimate Britain's imperial power" (Burt, 2003b, 17).

From performing for the ruling class and educated subalterns in Bombay and Calcutta as early as the 1770s interest in Shakespeare soon widened to the Indian bourgeoisie. The first Bengali playhouse, Hindu Theatre of Calcutta, opened in 1831 with a double bill of scenes from Julius Caesar and an English translation of a classic Sanskrit play. Further, the commercial 'Parsi theatres' that originated in Bombay and toured widely, performing in English or one of the Indian languages enhanced the Shakespearean influence much more. James Ivory's *Shakespeare Wallah* (1965) and Aparna Sen's *36 Chowringhee Lane* (1981) placed the new medium of Indian cinema in tension with the Shakespeare in the theatre or in schools. Utpal Dutt, a Bengali actor created a revolutionary popular theatre for working-class and rural audiences, relying upon the lively Bengali folk theatre called Jatra, adapting Shakespeare to the mythic life of villagers who had never seen themselves as part of the colonial world.

The multiple re-imaginings of Shakespeare's plays connote that Shakespeare's iconicity is manifested in an increasingly inter-, intra-, and multi-cultural global discourse. From among all the foreign writers none has captured the imagination of Indian filmmakers as William Shakespeare. The President of the South Asian Film Society, Snigdha Sur, traced in Shakespeare, "a lot of spectacle, a lot of stage props, surrealism and magic." She continues, "If there's any Western theater that should appeal to Indian audiences, it's Shakespeare." "Shakespeare has always influenced Bollywood more than people think because of the

Indian theater tradition, " Sur added. As actor Naseeruddin Shah affirms, "The roots may look lost but every big story in Hindi film industry is from Shakespeare…."

Shakespeare's entry into Indian cinema can be traced back to 1852, when the first performance of *The Taming of the Shrew* in Gujarati was held in Surat. *The Merchant of Venice* was translated into Tamil under the title *Venice Viapari, Hamlet* into Marathi as *Vikaravilasita* and *Khudadad*, an adaptation of *Pericles*, was performed by the Express Victoria Theatrical Company. Sohrab Modi's *Khoon ka Khoon* recreated *Hamlet* in his film, Amrit Rai translated *Hamlet* in Hindi and Gulzar based his movie *Angoor* on *The Comedy of Errors*. It is in the performances of Shakespeare on Indian stages in Indian theatrical forms, rather than in the classroom, that the response of India to Shakespeare can be best seen.

Rajiva Verma, in tracing the presence of Shakespeare in popular mainstream Bombay cinema from its early phase to the present, argues that Shakespeare's presence is "not as a cultural icon but as a resource to be exploited for characters and situations, often with our acknowledgement. They point to a greater complexity in the relationship between metropolis and periphery than postcolonial theory would seem to allow" (Verma 270).

According to Verma, "an audience brought up on a diet of Bombay films would find Shakespeare's plays, if it could read them, full of echoes from the films" (287). Since Bollywood has developed into "buzz word" in West Europe and the US over the last ten years most people are aware of the potential of hindi popular films.With changing demand patterns and new tastes, movies like Vishal Bhardwaj's *Omkara* (Othello), *Maqbool* (Macbeth) and Rituparno Ghosh's *The Last Lear* (King Lear), have recently ushered Shakespeare into Bollywood.

Maqbool (2004), based on Macbeth, and *Omkara* (2006), based on *Othello,* are the first Indian film adaptations of Shakespeare to have gained international recognition; they have been screened at several international film festivals and are discussed in Daniel Rosenthal's *100 Shakespeare Films* (2007), published by the British Film Institute. Bhardwaj has adapted both tragedies into a modern Indian setting, turning Macbeth into a gangster in Mumbai and Othello into a political enforcer. Vishal Bhardwaj's film can be seen as an attempt of post-colonial writing and therefore possible revision of Shakespeare's position within a post-colonial context.

In this paper, I would like to analyze Vishal Bhardwaj's adaptations of *Macbeth* and *Othello* and explore how he has moulded the bard's plays to fit in the contemporary commercial cinema without abandoning its quintessence.

Maqbool deftly blends the basic plot structure of Shakespeare's play with the increasingly popular genre of Bollywood gangland films. Set in the criminal underworld of modern-day Bombay, *Maqbool* opens with the prognostication of the witches of Shakespeare's play, reincarnated here as horoscope-touting policemen, foretelling the rise and ultimate destruction of Miya Maqbool, the principal henchman of Abbaji, the 'Duncan' figure in Maqbool, who stands in absolute contrast to the benevolent monarch in Shakespeare. The astrologer-cops and their prophecies, the recent troubles plaguing Mumbai's underworld indicated at the start of the story reminds us inevitably of the Shakespearean original. Abbaji's brother has been killed by a rival gang which spurs Maqbool to seek revenge on the offenders, reminding us of Macbeth who had similarly succeeded in crushing the Norwegian attacks. The ghosts of hover over the victorious lieutenants Maqbool [Macbeth] and Kaka [Banquo] who retreat to the farmhouse to await further orders. They happen to encounter Pandit and Purohit, who regale Maqbool with the brilliant prospects guaranteed by his astrological chart:

> *Pandit*: Your comet has entered the seventh position in your Venus chart. This position heralds your kingly reign. Forget Bollywood.... In six months, Abbaji's throne is going to be Miyan's. King of Kings.
>
> *Purohit*: Shut your trap, sonuvabitch.... Shut up.
>
> *Maqbool*: If I believed in any of this mumbo jumbo, Pandit, I would have sliced your tongue off right here.

Pandit predicts that Maqbool will soon control the gang's investments in Bollywood. Incredibly, the henchman overlooking Bollywood operations is soon revealed as a traitor, and Maqbool is appointed in his place. Kaka, his interest piqued, demands to know his fortune, as well. The cops skirt the question and instead, prophesy that Kaka's son, Guddu (Fleance) will be the antidote to Maqbool.

As prophesied, Maqbool manages to kill Abbaji, the head of a crime family who treats Maqbool as if he were his own son. Next, Maqbool falls passionately in love with Abbaji's mistress, Nimmi, who embodies an interesting reworking of Lady Macbeth, blending more powerfully than most other characters the Shakespearean and Bollywood influences of the film. While for Lady Macbeth the only motivation behind her crime was her over ambition, for Nimmi, murdering Abbaji meant much more than mere ambition or revenge. Instead, it was her love for Maqbool that instigates her. However, unlike Shakespeare's Lady Macbeth, Nimmi is feminine, her suggestions are whispered softly, and her desire for children is the core of her plan. Her pregnancy eventually ignites the desire of Maqbool to shoot Abbaji and the couple arranges the murder to appear to have been done by Abbaji's personal bodyguard. While Nimmi had resorted to insinuations earlier, she now explicitly goads Maqbool to murder. Wearing the sacrificial garland reserved for slaughtered goats, she exclaims:

> *Nimmi*: It's time you sacrificed me, too. Jahangir has got a new mistress. How can I face going home? Everyone knows I'm Jahangir's mistress. He looks disgusting with his clothes off. Must be my father's age.
>
> *Maqbool*: And he is my father. I've been brought up in this house.

Nimmi persists in her pleas for the murder. She informs Maqbool that he has to choose between two deaths—Abbaji's or her own. The murder therefore is triggered by ambition as well as love. Maqbool is strengthened in his resolve to kill Abbaji once he learns from the corrupt policemen that in all likelihood, Abbaji himself killed his mentor in order to head the gang. Consequently, after Abbaji himself is murdered, there is little doubt in anyone's mind that Maqbool is the killer, and the members of the gang soon regroup, isolating Maqbool in the process. Once the pair tacitly agrees on the deed, Maqbool begins to hallucinate. He cries out to his aged servant demanding that the blood from the morning's slaughter be cleaned up, only to be told that the stains had been washed away hours ago. Nimmi, on the other hand, appears to be more impervious to the moral consequences of the impending act. At night, Maqbool enters Abbaji's bedroom as Nimmi lies vigilantly beside the sleeping gang lord. The single shot that kills Abbaji also smears Nimmi with blood. Trapped inside the mosquito net, she tries to brush away the blood-splatter—a gesture that would later become the hallmark of her madness. The murdering duo pin the blame on an inebriated guard. His blood splashes over Nimmi, who like her Shakespearean counterpart, becomes increasingly obsessed with imaginary bloodstains.

Bhardwaj's adaptive genius translates the banquet scene into a meeting of Maqbool's gang, from which Guddu and Kaka (Fleance and Banquo) are missing. When Kaka's dead body is brought back, only Maqbool thinks that Kaka is alive and looking at him and so becomes visibly disturbed. Maqbool's fear of Kaka's gaze is tied to Abbaji's murder scene, in which Abbaji dies looking at Maqbool. Another brilliant reworking is the recasting of Macbeth's downfall with the foiling, by the port authorities, of Maqbool's attempt to offload contraband and the subsequent raid of his home. The policemen had predicted that Maqbool will be safe as long as the sea does not enter his house, Thus, the coming of the sea is the film's suggested parallel with Birnam Wood. The customs agents foil a vital smuggling deal at the port and raid Maqbool's home with the intention of arresting him. Instead, the customs agents find the dead body of Nimmi, who has, in the meanwhile, given birth to a child; whether it is Abbaji's or Maqbool's remains uncertain. When Maqbool, attempting to take his newborn son and flee the country, sees the child being taken care of by Guddu and Sameera at the hospital, he decides not to continue this life of violence and vengeance. Instead, as he emerges from the hospital, he is killed by Boti, another gangster who has joined with Guddu against Maqbool as their common enemy. In the memorable final shot, Maqbool's dying impressions are conveyed by a gradually reddening screen, as noises of commotion gradually fade into nothingness.

"No Shakespearean play," says Cartelli and Rowe in their recent *New Wave Shakespeare on Screen* (2007) "has been adapted to the screen as provocatively as *Othello* has in the last twenty years" (Cartelli and Rowe, 120). Orson Welles' *Othello* (1952) has been described as diminishing Othello's blackness through its black and white *filmnoir* approach. Laurence Olivier's *Othello* (1965) had to face severe criticism due to its "appalling projection of racist stereotypes" (Aebischer, 62): his Othello is visibly othered by a thick layer of black makeup, an 'African' voice, rolling eyes, a west Indian accent, "a vulgar, open mouthed, lipsmacking laugh and an inclination to sensuality" (Aebischer, 62f). Vishal Bhardwaj's *Omkara* convincingly integrates the bard's text into the conventions of Indian popular cinema and also alters these conventions through its revision of *Othello*. *Omkara* appropriates both Shakespeare's play and Bollywood conventions in order to create a contemporary *Othello* with truly international appeal.

Rooted in the setting of Uttar Pradesh, which not only accounts for the characters accent but also provides the messy setting of corrupt local politics. Omkara works for a local politician known as Bhaisaab, and supports him in his ruthless campaign for a parliamentary seat which entails the murdering of Bhaisaab's political opponents. Most of the action takes place in Omkara's home village, where he has taken his future bride Dolly, while they are waiting for an auspicious date for marriage.

Drama brews up when Omkara chooses Kesu Firangi (Vivek Oberoi) as his successor. Langda Tyagi, who was hoping to become Omi's second-in-command, is filled with envy. The seeds of Omkara's jealousy are sown when in "analogy to Shakespeare's play, Dolly's father warns him about his daughter's duplicity—"General [...] may you never forget the two faced monster a woman can be!" (0:20:41). As in Othello, Dolly is very innocent. Langda Tyagi, the film's Iago, is Omi's longtime friend, and brother-in-law. In his sinister plots, Langda instrumentalizes Raju, Dolly's former fiance and his wife Indu, and finally manages to make Omi believe that Dolly is having an affair with Kesu. He takes Rajan under his wing and plans to create a rift between Omi and Kesu. First, he gets Kesu drunk and involved in a brawl. Kesu's behaviour angers Omkara. Then, Langda convinces Kesu that the only way he can win back Omi's trust is through Dolly. Kesu requests Dolly to plead his case to Omkara. Omi and Langda return from a trip to find Kesu and Dolly alone in the house. To avoid facing Omi, Kesu runs away stealthily. This sows the seed of suspicion in Omi's head. Langda takes advantage of this and further poisons Omi's mind with well-crafted lies about a possible affair between Kesu and Dolly. But Omkara wants an evidence to clear away his doubts that Dolly is being unfaithful to him. That evidence comes in the form of a cummerbund that Omi had given to Dolly. Langda gets his wife Indu (Konkana Sen) to steal that cummerbund and later gives it to Kesu. When Omi sees the same cummerbund with Kesu's mistress Billo (Bipasha Basu), his fears are confirmed. Blinded by jealously, Omkara destroys his own world.

Thus, anchored in this genre micro-script, *Omkara* starts with an interrupted wedding and ends with a wedding that is followed by several deaths, while there is no staged wedding in *Othello*, only references to the interrupted first night in Cyprus and focus on the marriage bed, that, thought to have been polluted by the act of infidelity, becomes the scene of crime at the end. In *Omkara*, the time in-between the interrupted nuptial and the ill-fated wedding, through insistent and deft crosscutting, is linked to campaign activities of politicians and their gangster-activists who consistently use violent and criminal means to achieve political ends. Clearly, the changes Bhardwaj makes in the original story do not alter the basic plot line, nor crucial parts of dialogue that become nodes for plot transformation and changes in characters' moods, mood congruent emotions and mind set; he only changes the emotion micro-genres or scripts at critical moments.

However, there are a few small variations *Omkara* makes from *Othello*, as any such adaptation will have. Though the actions of Langda are quite similar to those of Iago in *Othello*, there are many apparent differences between the two; these differences combine in order to make the antagonist Langda a lesser villain than his counterpart, Iago, in *Othello*. The film achieves this by creating certain scenes which allow the audience to sympathize with Langda and by removing many of the aspects which show up in *Othello* which portray Iago as a conniving, scheming villain. Thus, in *Othello*, there is no sympathy felt for Iago, throughout the play. In *Omkara*, on the other hand, Langda is a character to which the audience has an ability to relate, even though he is seen performing evil actions. This is achieved by presenting Langda's motives for revenge in a more humane light. In the ritual where Langda is to choose his replacement, Langda, as well as others around him, believes that he will be chosen as the new general. Omkara hands Langda the ceremonial plate, and it seems as if he is about to place the beads on Langda, signifying his choice. At the last moment, however, Omkara turns to Kesu and appoints him as the new general. This choice is unexpected, both by the audience and by Langda, and the shot of Langda's fallen face, full of with disappointment and hurt, is meant to be deeply felt by the audience. This scene moves the viewer to sympathize with Langda, and feel as if Langda actually deserved to be appointed. Another way in which the viewer is led to sympathize with Langda arises from the film's depiction of Kesu's character. While Cassio, in *Othello*, is seen by the characters other than Iago as a courageous man who is able to fight, Kesu, in the film, is portrayed more as a smiling, charming man who does not belong in the place of a fighter. Next, whereas in *Othello*, Cassio seems to have been chosen rightly to be lieutenant, in *Omkara* there is special mention that the reason Kesu is appointed is not for his own merits but rather because he will draw the college students' votes. Kesu seems less worthy of the position of general than Cassio seems for that of lieutenant. When Kesu is appointed general; everyone is celebrating in a club, and Langda goads Kesu to drink, and when Raju smokes next to druken Kesu after being told not to, he begins beating up on Raju. In *Othello*, Roderigo tries to incite Cassio, but Cassio does not flare up at him. By showing Kesu's anger at Raju's trivial offence, Kesu seems less worthy of being general and Langda seems more justified in his claim. In *Othello*, Iago is seen from the beginning planning his revenge on Othello. Iago says about Othello, "Though I do hate him as I do hell's pains, Yet, for necessity of present life, I must show out a flag and sign of love which is indeed but sign" (1.1.153-56). In *Omkara*, it is not until later in the film that Langda decides to take action against Omkara. Only when Raju taunts Langda about the injustice done to him by Omkara when Kesu was chosen over him that Langda realizes that a wrong has been committed against him. It is only at this point that Langda appears to decide to do something about what Omkara has done. In *Othello*, an entire scene is devoted to Iago telling Roderigo that Desdemona is having an affair with Cassio, and explaining to him how to provoke Cassio in order to start a fight. In *Omkara*, Langda does not lie to Raju and tell him that Kesu and Dolly feel anything for each other. In addition, though it seems as if Langda does direct Raju to provoke Kesu, we do not hear what he tells him.

The film received high accolades from Philip French in *The Observer*, who called the adaptation "ingenious" and wrote the following: "Mobile phones are used where Shakespeare employed eaves dropping; an erotic, bejeweled waistband replaces the handkerchief as a compromising device." Peter Bradshaw remarked in *The Guardian*: "Vishal Bhardwaj's *Omkara* is a flawed but worthwhile attempt to transfer *Othello* to the modern setting of Uttar Pradesh in India and to render the story in a Bollywood style." Bradshaw also found the adaptation of *Othello* appropriate, because Bollywood, he added, "with its liking for ingenious fantasy and romance, has often seemed to me to resemble in style, nothing so much as a late Shakespearean play."

REFERENCES

Aibscher, Pascale, "Black Rams Tupping White Ewes" in *Retrovisions, Reinventing the Past in Film and Fiction*. Eds. Deborah Cartwell, I.Q. Hunter and Imelda Wheleham. London: Pluto, 2001. 59-73.

Burt, Richard and Lynda E. Boose, eds. *Shakespeare the Movie, II: Popularizing the Plays on Film, TV, Video, and DVD*. London and New York: Routledge, 2003.

Cartelli, Thomas and Katherine Rowe, *New Wave Shakespeare on Screen: Cultural Perception of Shakespeare*, Polity, 2007.

Kennedy, Dennis and Yong Li Lan (Ed.), *SHAKESPEARE IN ASIA—Contemporary Performance*, Cambridge University Press, 1993, 2.

Pavis, Patrice. *Theatre at the Crossroads of Culture*. Trans. Loren Kruger. London: Routledge, 1992.

Rothwell, Kenneth and Annabelle Henkin Melzer, *Shakespeare on Screen: An International Filmography and Videography*, New York: Neal Schuman, 1990.

Rushdie, Salman, *Imaginary Homelands,* London: Granta Books, 1991, p. 16.

Singleton, Brian. "Interculturalism." *The Oxford Encyclopedia of Theatre & Performance.* Ed. Kennedy (2003).

Tatlow Antony, *Shakespeare, Brecht, and the Intercultural Sign* (Durham, NC: Duke University Press, 2001, 5.

Verma, Rajiva. "Shakespeare in Hindi Cinema." *India's Shakespeare: Translation, Interpretation and Performance*. Ed. Poonam Trivedi and Dennis Bartholomeusz. Newark: University of Delaware Press, 2004. 269-90.

Worthen, W.B. *Shakespeare and the Authority of Performance.* Cambridge: Cambridge University Press, 1997.

❑❑❑

Chaplin's Aesthetics of Organic Dynamism and the Triumph of the Tramp

[A Tribute to Chaplin on 125th birth anniversary and 100 years of film making.]

DEBESH THAKUR

TIME was when 'photographic representation' was an expression of disapproval. Mechanical accuracy, it was supposed, dehydrates art of its staple, the imagination. This attitude has recently changed and film is no longer looked upon as untouchable in the temple of the Muses. This is because the great film-makers of the world have shown that even celluloid or digital representation of an object is not just mechanical. It is true that the process is mechanical, for in filming an image, the light reflected from an object is collected by a system of lenses and directed on to a sensitive plate called celluloid or digitally recorded. And yet the image reproduced mechanically is aesthetic because it is the imaginative eye of the cameraman or the director that selects the perspective or the angle of view which makes the image beautiful. In other words, the art of filming does not consist simply in bringing an object within camera-range. It is the angle and perspective which account for the depth dimension and de-familiarize the familiar. Hence when a picture of a train moves from the lower margin of the screen to the upper, we have an illusion of a train coming and then going away.

It is worth pointing out that though cinema is a form of visual art, it has an identity distinct from that of painting or photograph. A photograph, like painting, is 'still' but cinema is not fixed to a 'single mood.' It is a moving picture and hence it is called a 'movie'. When the period of silent cinematograph was over in 1928, for sometime the word 'talkie' became fashionable only to be replaced by 'movie' afterwards. It is sometimes argued that painting is superior to cinema as an art form, for reality in painting is filtered through the artist's imagination. But filming, as has already been pointed out, cannot be altogether mindless. Moreover, cinema has other advantages over painting. In painting the nearer objects are magnified dimensionally and the remoter objects are reduced in size. In both the cases the painter relativizes the size by actually distorting the object painted. In cinema, however, the object looks smaller or bigger but there is no actual distortion of shape as in painting. Besides, sound is a property in modern cinema which distinguishes it from the dumb world of painting. Not that speech is primary in this visual form of art; nevertheless it brings cinema closer to life. Chaplin may be inimitable in his pantomimes but minus the evocative power of the words much of the charm of *The Great Director* would have been lost. We may refer in this context to the use of background music in the films of Satyajit Ray. *Postmaster* picturises rural life. Hence, Ray creates valuable effect by using ordinary village musical instruments. On the other hand, the manorial sophistication in *Jalsaghar* (The Music Room) calls for richer music and this has been provided by the use of the classical notes on the sitar. Later on when sound helped the film to rise above the dumb world of painting, in absence of colour cinema was felt to be inferior to painting because the multi-coloured world would get reduced to a bi-chromatic world in a film. But ever since the shooting of *Becky Sharp* (1935), the first colour film of the world, cinema has come to rival, even dislodge the other art forms. Today, cinema is not, as alleged, theatre recorded in a video cassette/c.d. Like drama, film is also a 'collective' art to which the actor, the cameraman, the costumier, the light-man, the choreographer all contribute their mite. But whereas a theatre has to entirely depend on sets, that is, artificial location, in shooting a film the director may choose to replace sets by actual places. Furthermore, in a playhouse due to physical distance an object of enormous importance, like the dagger in *Macbeth*, cannot be foregrounded; in cinema it can be easily done by presenting a *close shot* of the dagger.

The film language is essentially visual. More clearly speaking, it is basically a camera language. Here the position of the camera plays a pivotal role in creating aesthetic impression. For example, the towering personality of a character may be symbolized through a shot taken from the worm's eye-view. In such a shot the camera looks up at him as at a mountain. Every director worth his salt uses there camera-tricks effectively. In *fast motion* films are shot at a slower speed than the normal and as such during projection at normal speed the motion accelerates. This device is used commonly for comic effects. Its opposite is *slow motion* in which over 250 shots are taken per second and consequently when they are projected at normal speed, the motion slows down. A sick man's movement may be effectively presented by using this camera technique even though the actor walked at normal speed. By *panning* the camera the spectator may be made to feel that a man is drunk or a victim of vertigo. In order to avoid sudden appearance film-makers allow objects to *fade in*, that is, to grow slowly out of darkness. *Fading out* in which an object dwindles out of sight, however, is used to suggest a break, as if the curtain has been dropped. In *dissolving* one shot melts into the other without a *cut*. Shots combined on the principle of similarity, say the flight of birds and of an aeroplane may be *dissolved* into each other. In *cut*, however, two separate shots are joined by film adhesive. How powerfully cut can be used to produce an effect is shown in Esienstein's *Strike*. There is a scene in which workmen on strike are being shot down. With a *cut* Eisenstein changes the scene to an ox-slaughter. The slaughtering of an ox and firing on striking hands thus become one in the symbolic frame. Another much used cut-device is *flashback* in which earlier happenings reviewed through memory or dream are inserted in the middle of the film. In *reverse shots* the camera is inverted for creating a certain illusion. Thus if Gupi Gyen and Bagha Bayen in *reverse shots* jump from a certain height, the spectator sees them vanish into the air. *Super imposition* or double exposure is employed mainly to put one shot on the other. Satyajit Ray uses it impressively in *Shakha Prasakha* (*A Family Tree*). Here the title is cast on a mobile cardiograph slide. This symbolizes the cardiac failure of a moribund society vivified through the mutual interaction of the members of a family. Directors often turn to this device when an actor appears in a double role in the same scene. A brilliant use of the technique is to be found in Ermler's *The Fragment of an Empire*. A German soldier and a Russian soldier attack each other and a close-up shows that their faces are identical. The double exposures finger at the folly of war which forces a man to turn upon himself in a different uniform.

Montage is another photographic technique in which sights disconnected in time and space are joined filmically to express a mood or to set a tone. Thus in Pudovkin's *Mother* the clippings of a smiling face, a rushing brook, a spring flower and sun rays are combined into a montage of 'joy'. The camera following a moving object on a trolley, known as *track shot,* can be made highly artistic. In Alexander Room's *The Ghost that Never Returns* a man is shown walking along a narrow corridor. Finding a flower which symbolizes liberty suddenly he raises his fist at the camera which is now rolled behind the prison bars. At once the identity of the man and his state of mind become clear to us. *Close-ups* and *long shots* are two other cinematographic styles which aestheticize a film. A *long shot* includes the whole of everything that is relevant to the particular total situation. A *close-up*, technically, is the picturing of a small detail which will not ordinarily be obvious in a long-shot; for example, a scar on a hand. Fusing *long-shot*s and *close-u*ps one can create an effect of perspective alteration. For example, in the film version of Ibsen's *A Doll's House* while taking a *long shot* of a house of standard size the camera simultaneously presents a *close-up* of a hand. As a result while the house gradually gets dwarfed the size of the hand gets enlarged on the screen. Thus an aesthetic impression is created that Nora's house is but a doll's house, which is fragile in nature. Use of *freeze* or the grafting of still photograph on a movie may be put to a highly artistic use. The ending of *Charulata* is an instance in point. Tagore's novel *Nastanir* (*The Spoilt Nest*) ends at a point where Charu rejects her husband's proposal of going to Mysore. In the film, the shot freezes before the extended hands of Charu and Bhupati touch each, thus conveying to us a suggestion of the futility of their reconciliation.

Over the years cinema as an art form has been fast maturing. The problem of back haziness which cinema could not tackle in its infancy has been removed through *deep focus*. Jean Renoir has pioneered in the use of *deep focus* in which the intensification of back lighting makes the front and the back equally distinct. Apart from this, the three milestones of its evolution are the transition from silent film to sound-cinema, from black and white to colour film and from celluloid to digital photography. While the use of Dolby soundtrack has brought about acoustic refinement in the art, improvement in colour composition, three dimensional projection system and switch from lengthy photo-tapes to digital microchip have almost revolutionized the art.

II

Since 1872, when John D. Isaacs made motion picture possible, cinema, the youngest of art forms, has grown from strength to strength. Though it is rather naïve to compare one form of art with another, for every form has its own rules, advantages and limitations, still in this heyday of interdisciplinary studies, it is common not only to make a comparative study of different art forms, but also to explore the possibility to integrate one form with another, so as to achieve richer results. Cinema has gained popularity particularly because of this: it can integrate all the possible advantages of painting, music, literary texts and the theatre. Therefore, cinema can easily aspire to ensure an aesthetic pleasure in a much more holistic way than any of its sister arts can.

But then, coming to the question of aesthetic pleasure, aesthetics itself has been defined and explained from various standpoints, some of them posited almost in binary relations, from the days of Plato on the one hand and Bharata on the other. Whatever might be the points of difference, the common objective in all these definitions is to see aesthetics as the study of beauty. However, much debate arose on the definition particularly by Marxian critics who showed that man's aesthetics connected more with social values and commitment than beauty. The involvement of a hungry man with the moon radically differs from that of newly-wedded couple. So, the study of beauty, as encouraged by aesthetics, should be supplemented by both internal and external feelings and sensibilities. When a connoisseur critically listens to the classical musical concerts, he may visualize sequence through his inner eye. On the other hand, a lover of art when engrossed in the beauty of Vinci's magnificent painting may hear the language of Jesus in course of his supper with his followers, though it is a visual art. Only external sense organs cannot judge the aesthetic unless supported by instinct and commitment.

In cinema one has a new art, the art of movement, an art based on that which is the very principle of everything that exists; an art which is the least conventional of all art, an immense visual orchestra on which the precursors were the masters of colours and brush—Michelangelo, Tintoretto, Rubens and many others. Cinema as an art form, is a near kin to painting, and moves and renews itself ceaselessly in a visible symphony into which the rhythm of the dance and the mysterious matrix of a musical poem coalesce to unite in course of time. In fact the mechanism of this art is so directed as to bring before man's eyes the whole universe of moving form, reconstituting it for a space in which time involves itself, after man has spiritualized and regulated it in his heart. Film is a new art which has less to do with the theatre. It is a mistake perhaps to associate it with plastic art. Elic Faure argues: "It is still inorganic, and will not find its true rhythm still society itself has found its rhythm. How then can we define it? It is still embryonic. A new art must create its own organs. All that we can do is to help to deliver them out of chaos" (Cited in Schickel 76).

A number of exponents have worked on the film-form, on its technology, text and texture, but only the greatest among them have successfully used the art form as a keyboard where all the elements of sense and feeling merge and convey in one cinematographic expression the complex revelation of their inner life and quality. They are the real masters of the art. They have no need even to mask an ephemeral gesture in the conventional manner of the mimic. In them the human drama possesses an instrument of expression to which people of the whole world can spontaneously respond. Nothing more is needed to draw from the heart a wave of new harmonics, a sudden realization of the inevitability of things, and the everlasting monotonous rhythm of the passions. For there, upon the cinema-screen, are forms that move, faces that reveal, a confused, continuous play of values, lights and shadows, composing and deconstructing unceasingly, uniting the impulses and desires which they express with the feelings and the ideas of the spectator. Charlie Chaplin surely is one of those few masters.

Charlie Chaplin, one of the greatest film-makers of his time and beyond, treated art as a measure for human values, social commitments and beauty. Aesthetics is a science of beauty; but Chaplin's films are more than what is merely beautiful, for his distinction as an artist lies in the art of fusing social commitment with pure entertainment which presupposes disinterestedness of aesthetic enjoyment. The fusion of these two irreconcilable poles of art and culture accounts for his outstanding position in the history of film. His excellence lies in the fact that he knew the art of organic dynamism which gave him a notable position. He had the mastery to organize various items and articles of art symmetrically and systematically. He knew the art of harmonization and orchestration of diverse materials—even materials which are apparently incompatible, into an organic order. From various standpoints, be it presentational and technical, Chaplin consciously and deliberately synchronizes every item in its optimum order. He knew how to organize acting, directing, pantomime, satire with the help of technical devices like camera, light, set design, music, sound and the like. This power of orchestration, however, is always dynamic and never static in Chaplin, for it grows as he matures as an interpreter of life and time.

Chaplin, the most popular art-exponent of his time, dealt with aesthetics from every possible aspect and thus he emerged as the creative genius in the history of film. He, however, remains the only film-maker to retain his outstanding position for decades and centuries. The views of some of Chaplin's contemporary film-makers and actors may be cited here in support of the observation. The Great Italian film director Federico Fellini claims that Chaplin, being the precursor of film-genesis is a "sort of Adam, from whom we are all descended…there were two aspects of his personality; the vagabond but also the solitary aristocrat, the prophet and the poet" (Robinson 631). Rene Clair, doyen of the French cinema, wrote that Chaplin was "a monument of the cinema of all countries and all times" (Robinson 631). Another French film-maker and comedian Jacques Tati said, "His work is always contemporary, yet eternal" (Robinson 631). Laurence Olivier, great Shakespearean actor, said, 'He was perhaps, the greatest actor of all time,' whereas Jean-Louis Barrault described him as "the supreme example of the perfection of the actor and the creative genius […]. In sum he has shown us the peak of art of mime" (Robinson 632).

Another example of his outstanding popularity, though crude and cruel, may be noted in this context. Chaplin died peacefully in his sleep in 1977 in the small hours of Christmas Day, and was cremated on 27 December, 1977 at the Anglican Church in Vevey, Switzerland. After two months of his funeral, Chaplin, with his taste for the macabre, might have found an ideal scenario in the bizarre events when on 2nd March 1978 the superintendent of the Vevey cemetery found Chaplin's grave opened up and the coffin gone. Within a few days it became evident that it was a clear case of kidnapping as the first telephone call demanded 600,000 Swiss francs for the return of the body. Ultimately the coffin was found buried in a cornfield some twenty kilometres from Vevey. Unimportant as it may seem, the incident demands particular attention for it clearly, though in a bizarre manner, points to Chaplin's undying popularity even after his death.

Till 1922, during his contract with Key Stone, Essanay, Mutual Films and First National Films, Chaplin had little to do justice to his genius. From 1923 onwards when he came to be associated with the United Artists his genius erupted like a volcano; his excellence sprouted from all dimensions. From 1923 to 1957 he directed nine films (whereas thirty-five were produced in a single year, 1914)—*A Woman of Paris*, 1923, *The Gold Rush*, 1925, *The Circus*, 1928, *City Lights*, 1931, *Modern Times*, 1936, *The Great Dictator,* 1940, *Monsieur Verdoux* 1947, *Limelight*, 1953, *The King in New York*, 1957. In these and in *A Countess from Hong Kong* directed in 1971 his organic dynamism reached its peak.

Charlie Chaplin is the first man to create a drama that is purely cine-plastic, in which the action does not illustrate a sentimental fiction or moralistic intention but creates a monumental whole; projecting from the inner consciousness a personal vision of the object in a form that is actually material and perceptible. There, as it seems, we have something very great, an achievement comparable with Titan's concentration of all the sound-elements in time, thus creating it before us. Elic Faure's remark on the issue is worth quoting:

> Apparently most people do not perceive this because Chaplin is a clown, and because a poet is, by definition, a solemn person who brings us to knowledge through the door of boredom. Yet to me Chaplin is a poet, even a great poet, a creator of myths, symbols, and ideas, the discoverer of a new and unknown world. (Cited in Schickel 77)

Elic Faure is extremely sensitive to Chaplin's art form, a rare and inimitable form: "Indeed I do not know, for it is too essential to be defined. Every time I see him I have a sense of equilibrium and of certitude which liberates my judgment and sets my ideas swarming. Chaplin reveals to me what is in me, what is the truest in me, what is most human" (Cited in Schickel 77).

III

Now we may go deeper into the comparative study of film and literature to get some basic points that are important for Chaplin's films. Chaplin himself has this to say in this connection:

> Marc Connelly, the playwright, once posed the question: what should an author's approach be in writing for the theatre? Should it be the intellectual or the emotional? I think primarily emotional, because it is more interesting in the theatre than intellect, the theatre is designed for it, its rostrum, its proscenium, its red curtains, its whole architectural flounce is addressed to the emotion. Naturally intellect participates but it is secondary. Chekhov knew this; so did Molńar and many other play wrights. They also knew the importance of theatricalism, which is basically the art in playwriting. (*Autobiography* 273)

To Chaplin theatre means dramatic establishment: the art of aposiopesis; the abrupt closing of a book, the lighting of a cigarette, the effects off-stage, a pistol shot, a cry, a fall, a crash, an effective entrance, an effective exit—all of which may seem cheap and obvious, but if treated sensitively and with discretion, they are the poetry of the theatre.

Chaplin's primary concept of literature as film and film as literature has a distinct mark. Critics explained a lot to find out the difference and resemblance of literature and film. There is no denying the fact that these two art forms are close to each other. In this connection, Mohit K. Ray once observed that literature is as old as human civilization while film as a modern art form had its origin only in the beginning of the last century. One can film anything under the sun, any animate or inanimate object, any natural scenario or an event. That is not our immediate concern. We are concerned with the situation when a film is made out of a literary work. Mohit K. Ray goes further:

> There are many similarities between a literary work and a film. Both, for example, tell stories and are engaged in the act of communication. Both try to project the fabric of a vision and communicate a message to the reader/spectator. But the differences are many. The most important difference consists in the use of the medium. Literature is verbal, the film is visual. Literature is conceptual and discursive while film is perceptual and presentational. But the objective of both is the same: both want to make the reader/spectator see life. Conrad said in the preface to *The Nigger of the Narcissus*, "My task which I am trying to achieve is, by the power of the written word, to make you hear, to make you feel, it is, before all, to make you see." (Mohit K. Ray)

Film critics point out that the 'language' of film is exclusively different from the language of literature. While a literary work deals with literary texts, a film-maker uses lot of icons to establish the language of film: light, sound, scenario, camera, music, dialogue and so on. A literary work has certain advantages which a film does not have. An author can use his narrative power to describe the mental condition of a character in a particular situation he/she is placed in and there is no limit to the words. A literary work can run into volumes like Marcel Proust's *In Search of Time Lost,* Fielding's *Tom Jones* or Thomas Mann's *The Magic Mountain*. But a film cannot run for hours on end, and it can certainly never be as long as a voluminous literary work. The film script of *Moby Dick* runs to just hundred and fifty odd pages while the actual novel runs to more than one thousand pages.

Chaplin learnt the language of film from his parents, ancestors as well as from his instinct. He appears less traditional and more an individual talent in his application of aesthetics in films. Since we propose to deal with the last part Chaplin's film career when he was at the height of his maturity, we shall try to understand his organic dynamism as reflected in its multi-dimensional aspects. Chaplin says: "It seems that each time art is discussed I have a different explanation of it. Why not? […] art is a feeling more than a belief" (*Autobiography* 390).

When the greatest award from French Government 'Legion of Honour' was conferred on Chaplin, Mr. Roger Ferdinand, the President of *Société des Auteurs et Compositeurs Dramatiques,* wrote a letter touching upon the spirit of dynamism:

> You are among greatest personalities of the world and your claim to fame is equal to that of those who can be placed among most illustrious.
>
> There is your genius, for a start. This much abused word genius, takes on its real sense when applied to a man who is not only a marvelous comedian, but also an author, composer, producer, and, best of all, a man of warmth and magnanimity. For you are all these, and, best of all a man of warmth and moreover with a simplicity which increases your stature and makes a warm, spontaneous appeal, without calculation or effort to the hearts of many today, which are as tormented as your own. But genius is not sufficient to merit esteem, neither it is sufficient to endanger love. And yet love is the only word for the sentiment you inspire.
>
> When we saw *Limelight* we laughed, often heartily, and wept with real tears, for you gave us the precious gift of tears. (*Autobiography* 508)

Ferdinand expresses that the victory of Chaplin is in the fact that he has human generosity and spontaneity that are not inhibited by rules or cleverness but stem from his own sufferings, his joys, hopes and disappointments; all that is understood by those who suffer beyond their strength and ask for pity and who constantly hope to be comforted, to be made to forget for a moment, by the laughter which does not pretend to cure, but only to console. He has, Ferdinand recollects, by his talent alone, subdued the critics because he has succeeded in captivating them. This is a difficult task. They will never admit that he responds equally to the charm of old fashioned melodrama and to the devilish jest of Feydeau.

And yet he does, while also possessing a certain grace that makes one think of de Musset—although he imitates no one and resembles no one. That is the secret of his glory.

Thus the visual art changes essentially from the verbal art with the change from one medium to another. Literature possesses more freedom whereas a film is to compromise a lot as economy is integrally related to the production. Neither a director nor a cinematographer can take liberty with his script ignoring the commercial viability as a lot of money is involved in the project. They do not have the freedom to go on elaborating a point either. The film never acts as an analysis, it only suggests through symbols, visual data, metaphors, body of commentary, a one-eyed camera lens with sharp vision. Every lively item in a film, in fact, is organically and aesthetically interrelated with utmost dynamism. The uninterrupted course of life is the primary object of a movie. It is photography of life in motion, not a snapshot. In *The Gold Rush*, Chaplin, in quest of gold, reaches a place without life. Nobody enquires of the location, rather they are satisfied enough to see a pole-bear, the only living object in the dead land of snow. While a novelist would resort to an elaborate description of the sequence the film uses only a few organic symbols and suggestions. This is possible only through the artist's extreme command over the art form. A master film-maker, therefore, is capable of an organic mechanism to communicate and convey his vision. One may remember in this connection *Jalsaghar*, a story by Tarashankar Bandyopadhyay and filmed by Satyajit Ray. The scenario is built upon a short story of fourteen and a half pages. The short story requires less than an hour to go through. Satyajit Ray uses a number of details through symbols to establish the sequences. The faded light, oil paintings covered with cobwebs, ruins of the palace, gold coins, an insect in the glass of wine—every item is integrated and dynamically organized into an artistic whole. The text and the texture are so identically established that the short story achieves the form of an epic in the film version. The mastery of a writer and the 'language' of a great film-maker are intermingled substantially. Experience tells that the subtlest of emotional states affects a person's speech and behaviour and such revealing speech and behaviour is at the very heart of cinema's eloquence. He thought that it was a shrewd mood on his part to have selected for first film a story where one had to put the emphasis on the human aspect. He had also to take care of the technical points to appear refreshingly original. But balancing of means and ends is not an easy job, and a certain importance sometimes makes a director plunge into a subject that is clearly beyond his scope. This is how the exterior, the location, and the interior, the treatment and texture reached its height through his outstanding aesthetics of organic dynamism.

Another important question raised by critics in connection with aesthetic dynamism is the importance of form or content, which is prior and foremost in art and it may be discussed here. David Bordwell and Kristin Thompson throw light on this issue and say that very often people assume that 'form' as a concept is the opposite of something called 'content'. This implies that a poem or musical piece or a film is like a jug; an external shape, the jug, contains something that could just as easily be held in a cup or a pail. Under this assumption, form becomes less important than whatever it is presumed to contain. One may not accept this assumption. Considering form as the total system of the film implies that there is no inside or outside. We assume that every component functions within the overall pattern. Thus, we shall treat as formal elements many things that some people consider 'content'. From this standpoint, subject matter and abstract ideas all enter into the total system of the artwork. "They become related to one another and interact dynamically. As a result, subject matter and ideas become different from what they might be outside the work" (Bordwell and Thompson 28). This aesthetic instinct gives Chaplin a permanent place in the history of international film. From 'language' of film we may move towards the necessary steps taken in course of the making of a film as well as its comparative detachment from literature.

A film-maker is always concerned about the length and duration of the shooting. It must be remembered that all the shots taken for a film are never screened. For example, Chaplin's *The Kid*, the six-reel film, was screened after the editing of over 400,000 feet of film shoot which consisted of five hundred rolls. Over two thousand takes were sorted out. After shooting, editing is graded to be the most important part of film-making. To strike a balance between entertainment and commercial success is also one of the prime considerations of a successful film-maker. Every producer and distributor is concerned about the huge amount of investment and its feedback. Production and box office are essential terms eventually used by the investors and these act as the major criteria for most of the major films of Chaplin.

In course of the comparative study one should keep in mind that literature is always a simpler medium than the cinema for projecting the complexity and density of life. On the other hand, film is linked with painting and photography, two major art forms that reflect the emotion of real life. The treatment is kinetic and never static. Literature, being a conceptual and discursive form, uses words to tell a story; film being a perceptual and presentational form, uses images to establish the story or an idea. The aim of these two distinct media is almost same; to see life. Two films may be referred to discuss the vision of the directors who had *seen life* from different aspects: panoramic vision as in Griffith's *The Birth of a Nation* (1915, USA) and *The Bicycle Thief*, a bird's-eye view by Vittorio de Sica (1948, Italy). The first one is based on the story of Thomas Dixon during American Civil War (duration about three hours, shots 1375). This epical film stands as a milestone in the history of cinema till today. Filmed at a cost of one hundred thousand dollars, the three hour epic was enormously popular and equally controversial; it is still regarded as one of the key films in cinema history. *The Birth of a Nation* combines documentary re-enactments of historical moments such as Sherman's march to the sea and Lincoln's assassination with the fictitious story of two families' experiences during the war and the subsequent period of Reconstruction. The story evolves round the happy Camerons and the Stoneman children of Pennsylvania. The war inflicts suffering on both families, but after the fighting ends, the woes of the Camerons and their Southern neighbours increase. Kenneth S. Leish describes:

> Although Griffith's view of history and race relations was deplorable, his artistry was undeniable. It was as critic Bosley Crowther has written "as though a super symphony had burst from the muck of primitive music within two decades after the invention of the horn [...]. People were simply bowled over by its vivid pictorial sweep, its arrangements of personal involvements, its plunging of the viewer into a sea of boiling historical associations". (Leish 24)

The essence of organic dynamism is found in the way of seeing life on a big panorama; the epical treatment and state-of-the-art use of technological devices. Let us consider *The Bicycle Thief*, an Italian film of a tiny background. Leish observes the film as a "story of a poor billposter's search for the stolen bicycle that is essential to his job; it is also a tender, sensitive exploration of the man's relationship with his young son and a revealing depiction of a self-absorbed urban society" (Leish 125).

A number of world class film-makers were working outside the arena of Hollywood and producing outstanding films of aesthetic subtlety out of literary texts. Mention may be made of Sergei Eisenstein (Russia), François Truffaut (France), De Sica (Italy), Costa-Gavras (Algeria), Federico Fellini (Italy), Ingmar Bergman (Sweden), Akira Kurosawa (Japan), Jacques Tati (France), Jiri Menzel (Czechoslovakia). Even after fifties outstanding film-makers from India like Satyajit Ray, Ritwik Ghatak, Mrinal Sen introduced new approaches to 'see life' from the orient.

Two art forms, which basically aim to 'see life,' are restricted to some preconditions. The approach may be different, but the object is almost the same. Film combines many other forms of traditional art. Like ballet film relies heavily on movement and music; it presents a narrative depicting characters in a series of conflicts; like painting it also relies on light, shadow and sometimes colour. Literature and film base upon different mode of production, different censorship, different commercial viability and appeal. Literature is nothing but a process of concretization of a concept, just the starting point and the point of departure. A very good example may be the film version of Hemmingway's *A Farewell to Arms*. The director, in working with the theatrical art of attachment and detachment, shows great mastery. It underplays the love story and overemphasizes the war plot. Another good example is *Gupi Bain, Bagha Bain* (*Gupi the Singer and Bagha the Drummer*) by Satyajit Ray. Satyajit enjoyed enough freedom as he was working with the story of his grandfather, Upendrakishore. The story was originally intended for children and is told in the fairytale manner having a happy ending. Satyajit re-narrates the story so as to cater to the interest of children as well as the adult world. The author's lucid and simple narrative takes on a different dimension altogether in the film version. Satyajit Ray's primary language is akin to his grandfather's aesthetics but the method of concretization is different.

Charles Chaplin, unlike Ray, inherited more freedom than many others as he himself played the role of the protagonist; he was the author and script-writer, the director and sometimes the producer. He acquired the quality since the days in London when he joined the opera of Fred Karno. He had the conviction that he was out and out an artist. He had to undergo lot of financial troubles from his very childhood. He saw poverty, experienced hunger and sufferings. A mere child, he had been virtually compelled to earn a living by working in ten different capacities: flower-seller, worker in a chandler's shop, a doctor's boy, a page-boy in Lancaster Gati, news-agent for W.H. Smith and Son, a glass-blower, worker at Starker's printing and stationery shop, seller of old cloths, boat-maker, wood-chopper. But Chaplin's dream was not for existence but for living; living the life of an artist. From those days of joining with Karno, till 1914, his settlement with Keystone, his long cherished ideas started to bloom. In his teens he felt that his attachment to the industry is a history: "Thus grew a belief in myself that, I was creative and could write my own stories" (*Autobiography* 147).

This deep rooted belief, dynamic vision and organic texture are properties of Chaplin's films. His total film career may be divided into five stages: The Keystone Films (1914, 35 short films), The Essany Films (1915, 1916, 1918, 15 short films), The Mutual Films (1916, 1917, 12 films), The First National Films (1918, 1919, 1920, 1922, 1923, 9 films) and The United Artists Films (All full-length, 1923-57, 9 films). While in 1914 he made thirty-five short films in a single year, he later took thirty-four years to make only nine films.

Before going to the details of Chaplin's films it would perhaps be pertinent to go through the points and criteria Chaplin wanted to establish through his own experiments with different aspects of film-making: "If the amateur is creative, he needs only the barest technical essentials. To an artist, complete freedom to do the unorthodox is usually most exciting, and that is why many a director's first picture has freshness and originality" (*Autobiography* 250).

In this connection we may discuss in detail Chaplin's treatment of various devices necessary for the construction of a film. The intellectualizing of line and space, composition, tempo, is all very well, but it has little to do with acting, and is liable to fall into arid dogma. Simplicity of approach is always best. Personally Chaplin loathes tricky effects, photographing through the fireplace from the viewpoint of a piece of coal, or travelling with an actor through a hotel lobby as though escorting him on a bicycle; to him they are facile and obvious. As long as an audience is familiar with the *set*, it does not want the tedium of a travelling smear across the screen to see an actor move from one place to another. Such effects slow up action, and are boring and unpleasant, and have been mistaken for that tiresome word art.

Chaplin's efficiency in technology especially in camera set up is based on facilitating choreography for the actor's movements. When a camera is placed on the floor or moves about the player's nostrils, it is the camera that is giving the performance and not the actor. The camera should not obtrude the performance. Time-saving in films is still the basic virtue. Both Eisenstein and Griffith knew it. Quick cutting and dissolving from one scene to another are the dynamics of film technique. Chaplin asserts,

> I am surprised that some critics say that my *camera technique* is old-fashioned, that I have not kept up with the times. What times? My technique is the outcome of thinking for myself, of my own logic and approach; it is not borrowed from what others are doing. If in art one must keep up with the times, then Rembrandt would be a back number compared to Van Gogh. (*Autobiography* 251)

Chaplin seems particular in the subject and theme of his plays when he says that for the subject of films, a few brief words may be profitable for those contemplating making a super-duper special—which, as a matter of fact, is the easiest picture to make. It requires little imagination or talent in acting or directing.

The theme of most of these traditional sights is the superman. The hero can out-jump, out-climb, out-shoot, out-fight and out-love anyone in the picture. In fact every human problem is solved by these methods, except thinking. Chaplin discusses elaborately on the actor's role that in handling actors in a scene, psychology is most helpful. For instance a member of the cast may join the company in the middle of a production. Although an excellent actor, he may be nervous in his new surroundings. This is where a director's humility can be very helpful, as Chaplin had often found under these circumstances. "Although knowing what I wanted, I would take the new member aside and confide in him that I was tired, worried and at a loss to know what to do with the scene. Very soon he would forget his own nervousness and try to help me and I would get a good performance out of him" (*Autobiography* 253).

For theatrical sense and theatrical trick Chaplin seems sensitive as he says that an idea without *theatrical sense* is of little value. It is more important to be effective. With a theatrical sense one can be effective about nothing. In those days prologues went with all feature pictures and lasted about half an hour. Chaplin had no script or story but he remembered a sentimental, colour print captioned 'Beethoven's Sonata', depicting an artistic studio and a group of bohemians sitting moodily about in half-light, listening to a violinist. So he reproduced the scene on the stage, having only two days to prepare it. He engaged a pianist, a violinist, apache dancers and a singer, and then utilized every *theatrical trick* he knew. Guests sat around on settees or on the floor with their backs to the audience, ignoring them and drinking Scotch, while the violinist poured out his sonata, and in a musical pause a drunk snored. After the violinist had played, the apache dancers had danced, and the singer had sung *Après de ma Blonde* two lines were spoken. When the last had gone, the host lit a cigarette and began turning out the lights of the studio as voices were heard singing down the street *Après de ma Blonde*. When the stage had darkened, except for the moonlight streaming in through the centre window, the host exited and, as the singing grew fainter, the curtain slowly descended. Chaplin says that during this nonsense one could have hear a pin drop from the audience. For half an hour nothing had been said, nothing but a few ordinary vaudeville acts taken place on the stage. Yet on the opening night the cast took nine curtain calls. "I cannot pretend to enjoy *Shakespeare* in the theatre. My feeling is too contemporary. It requires a special panache type of acting which I do not like, and in which I am not interested. I fell I am listening to a scholarship oration" (*Autobiography* 254).

Chaplin liked the conventional theatre, with its proscenium that separates the audience from the world of make-believe. He liked the scene to be revealed by the lifting or parting of curtains. He disliked plays that come over the footlights and participate with an audience, in which a character leans against the proscenium and explains the plot. Besides being didactic, this device destroys the charm of the theatre, and is a prosaic way of getting over exposition. In *stage décor* Chaplin prefers that which contributes reality to the scene and nothing more. If it is a modern play of everyday life, he did not want geometric design which destroys make-believe. Some very fine artists have used their scenic effusions to the degree of subordinating both the actor and the play. On the other hand, just curtains and sets running up into infinity are worse intrusions. His feeling for sensible imagination receives a dimension when he said that he once saw Laurence Olivier in evening dress recite an excerpt from *Richard III* at a benefit. Although he achieved a medieval mood by his histrionics, his white tie and tails were rather incongruous.

Chaplin seems critical when he says that the basic principle of aesthetics can be applied to all the arts, but an actor especially must have restraint and an inner containment. No matter how frenzied the scene, the technicians are; the actor should be calm and relaxed. Only through relaxation can an actor achieve this. "My own method is rather personal: before going on the stage, always extremely nervous and excited, and in this state I get so exhausted that by the time I make my entrance I am relaxed" (*Autobiography* 253).

Chaplin never believed that acting can be taught. He had seen intelligent people fail at it and dullards act quite well. But acting essentially requires feeling: 'All intellect and no feeling can be characteristic of the arch criminal and all feeling and no intellect exemplifies the harmless idiot. But when intellect and feeling are perfectly balanced, then we get the superlative actor' (*Autobiography* 253).

Chaplin confesses that he knew little about the *method school of acting*. He understood that it concentrates on development of personality —which could very well be less developed in some actors. After all, acting is pretending to be other people, an imitation of one's day-to-day activities and feelings. Personality is an indefinable thing that shines through a performance in any case. But there is something to all methods. Stanislavski, for example, strove for 'inner truth'. This requires empathy, a felling into things: one should be able to feel what it is like to be a lion or an eagle, also to feel a character's soul instinctively, to know under certain circumstances what his reactions will be. This part of acting cannot be taught. In instructing a true actor or actress about a character, a word or a phrase will often suffice: "This is Falstaffian or this is a modern Madame Bovary". The theory that one must know a character's life story is unnecessary. Chaplin rejected dramatic schools that indulge in reflections and introspections to evoke the right emotion. The mere fact that a student must be mentally operated upon is sufficient proof that he should give up acting.

Chaplin's view of the truth of acting differs from the contemporary schools; to him orientation deserves special notice as he says that much-touted metaphysical word *truth* have different forms and one truth is as good as another. The classical acting at the Comédie Françoise is as believable as the so-called realistic acting in an Ibsen play; both are in the realm of artificiality and designed to give the illusion of truth—after all, in truth of acting there is the seed of falsehood. Even the beginner with talent must be taught technique, for no matter how great his gifts, he must have the skill to make them effective.

He had found that orientation is the most important means of achieving the success for an actor. Walking into a scene one must have the authority of knowing where to stop; when to turn; where to stand; when and where to sit; whether to talk directly to a character or indirectly. "Orientation gives authority and distinguishes the professional from the amateur. I have always insisted on this method of orientation with the cast when I'm directing my films" (*Autobiography* 254).

Chaplin wanted to indulge in very common and simple feelings of aesthetics. It was his experience of life rather than philosophy that nourished him into his creations. His experience with human life and human characters invoked within him the sense of art as he postulated: "There is no mystery connected with 'making people laugh'. All I have ever done is to keep my eyes open and my brain alert for any facts or incidents that I could use in because without a knowledge of it I could not do my work […] a knowledge of human nature is at the foundation of almost all success" (*Autobiography* 256). In course of his dealing with human nature he stressed upon two primary aspects—contrast and jerk. For contrast, Chaplin feels that to the average person contrast spells interest, and because it does he constantly makes use of it in his pictures: "by the contrast between big and little, I get the sympathy of audience and always I try to contrast my seriousness of manner with the ridiculousness of the incident" (*Autobiography* 257). Whenever Chaplin is dealing with any comical element he trusts more on contrast: tiny with titanic, thick with thin, talkative with mum. A comparative study of the barber and the dictator in *The Great Dlctator* may be placed here. He finds contrast as the prime of dramatic consequence. Viewers are never given ample time to stable with a particular idea for ever; ideas are shifted through various images. Construction of images and splitting up, moulding and re-moulding of emotion are juxtaposed aesthetically. Previously it was believed that grotesque is the origin of Chaplin's treatment. This is however a very timid experience; Chaplin studied human nature and character as through a microscope, dissected its aspects and placed then accordingly. Thus he felt life from contrast, conflict and pathos, and all his clowning was virtually based on this perception of life.

Chaplin's views on art are clear here. He stood apart from other film-makers who dealt with comical and seriocomic elements on the basis of consciousness. Chaplin is not such an idiosyncratic fool as he projects his tramp. In all comedy business, he feels, an attitude is all important.

Even he is more critical to denote, "you cannot be funny without an attitude. Being funny without an attitude in comedy is like something amiss in one's make up" (*Autobiography* 227).

Chaplin was aware of the traditional uses of comedy as a lesser art, as it is often used for buffoonery. In those cases, it engages itself only with cheap absurdities, idiosyncrasies and stock-of-the-trade situations. Chaplin consciously chose to be different. He had the firm belief that discrepancy or incongruity stands far away from 'logical action'. His comedy achieves the attainment as the outcome of sheer 'legitimate motivation'. It is more complex than farce, more relevant than discrepancy: "It is the subtle discrepancy we discern in what appears to be normal behaviour, through humour we see in what seems rational the irrational, in what seems important the unimportant [...] in an overstatement of seriousness lurks the absurd" (*Autobiography* 155).

The outstanding feature of Chaplin's art is that he never distinguished comedy from tragedy so far as the seriousness involved in them is concerned. His mastery lies in his treatment of the most trifle with titanic sympathy. Those common critical and analytical notes of comic relief take a very unusual form in Chaplin's aesthetics. He is aware of the view that they are more sympathetic while they laugh, and the minute a thing is over tragic, it is funny. Though Chaplin's aim is attachment of reason into comedy, finally he never sticks to mere reasons. Reasons and sensibility are juxtaposed together as he believes in fundamental senses which upgrade his art into the realm of aesthetic height. This sensibility may be treated as bourgeois sentiment but he feels great art is a feeling which cannot readily be defined. All of us who are healthy are born with same emotions and we will react to the appeal of beauty in much the same way. One may not have much patience with a thing of beauty that must be explained to be understood. Art is not only a study. It is beauty which gives joy and entertainment. It is a matter of feeling. His idea may also be supplemented with the idea that film creates emotion through eyes. It arouses emotions in a direct way. Of all mediums of art, it seems to be most direct. It translates, denotes and suggests emotions which convey beauty. Rudolf Arnheim clarifies that all media has multiple uses, only one of which is aesthetic, but it is this artistic function which generally makes us focus on the medium itself, thus poetry returns us to words, not to messages, and painting focuses our sensibilities on line, colour composition and other formal properties rather than on representation. Film-art likewise returns us to the basis of the medium rather than emphasizing the world it pictures. Most theorists have held that in some sense cinema is the medium of reality even if it is the displacement of the real. Probably Chaplin is the first exponent of this cinematic reality.

Chaplin's film is essentially architectural in its construction. Each scene is determined by Chaplin's conception of the whole, just as the smaller cupolas surround the great central cupola in the old Byzantine churches, or as music ordains the song of the spheres and controls the continuous harmony of their motion. In this respect, he is differentiated from the ordinary comedian—who is but an interpreter of ideas, sentiments. He himself combined the painter, the architect, or the musician, by the camera, the film, the screen, the colours, the brushes, the canvas, the compass as the instruments of the orchestration or organic dynamism. Like a painter, an architect, or a musician, Chaplin enters victoriously into the empire of poets. Elic Faure seems analytical and vivid when a comparison between Shakespeare and Chaplin is presented:

> I have said elsewhere that Chaplin makes me think of Shakespeare, and I repeat it, though doubtless many people will regard my insistence with scornful smile, for this impression forces itself upon me everything I see him. [...] If Chaplin leans towards the side of laughter, as Shakespeare does towards the side of lyrical ecstasy, it is again like Shakespeare, to evade vexatious reality. (Cited in Schickel 81)

It should be noted that Chaplin's dealing with art is basically depending on personal acting, primarily mime, having deep-rooted impact on universal acceptability. Sound track might have been a bar to this universalization of art. It is however a boundless journey towards humanity.

Recognition of human values stands as the *sine qua non* of Chaplin's aesthetics. Common mass, having no boundary of polarization of language, cult, custom, creed, comes to his movies as the universal existence; and we have a peaceful journey of commitment, in a candid way, with popularly accepted art form. This was achieved from his personal experience in those grief-stricken past and power of keen observation; he selected those variations and contrast of the nature of mankind as his raw materials.

Chaplin knew well that a class-divided society is based on contrasts between normal and abnormal, known and unknown. The tramp never fits in the existing system, reacts in a very unusual way, reflects in a way which seems abnormal, and contradicts what otherwise looks natural.

Chaplin's tramp is a composition of many Englishmen, with small black moustaches, tight fitting clothes and bamboo canes. This iconic figure of Chaplin becomes the representative of silent comedy. In those days the tramp was projected as a villain. For example, in Griffith the tramp represents a threat to the middle-class family, steals money, kidnaps basics and the like. Chaplin's tramp is a vagabond, an underdog whom the audience can sympathize with. Like the court jester or the Shakespearean fool, the tramp, as a social commentator, points out society's idiosyncrasies without malice:

> Chaplin's comedies inter-relate serious social issues with humorous situations creating a plethora of avenues for the tramp to do what he does best. Chaplin's tramp is naively ingenious in his ability to ascertain society's loopholes, physically adept at escaping society's traps, and above all else, the tramp is a hero to society's outcasts. (http//www.yahoo.com/an-analysis-comedia-contribution-Charlie-Chaplin.abstracted on 12 November, 2012.)

Chaplin's characterization of the tramp with cane and hat, boots and tatters, is, Elic Faure points out, as unchangeable as the mask and the 'cothurnus of the Greek drama'. His walk possesses such a musical rhythm, of his protruding feet, of his leaps of jubilation and light heartedness of his despairing staggering on one heel, "of his sudden turns at right angles, of his particular steps in moments of danger or when he is fighting, of the silhouette of this droll mechanical clown before which all humanity shakes with laughter" (Cited in Schickel 83).

Chaplin's expressions are very much personal, simple and sensible. He is keen to study the response of his viewer to his films. An artist generally projects his personal feelings and attitudes which may not always have a strict class-dimension. A great artist creates his own definition of the aesthetics. On the other hand, personal views are reflected here to classify some social existence; Chaplin has all along prioritized a person over the society. He also refuses to be defined by any political boundary. He was categorically against the imposition of any social view of an individual. On this aspect his stand and observation are exclusively different from his contemporary film-makers; his opinions are closer to the great exponents of world culture. Mention may be made of Roman Rolland, Albert Einstein and Rabindranath Tagore. We may quote two remarks by Chaplin in this context. When the US immigration department asked him whether he had any link with the communists, he replied, "I haven't joined a political organization in my life" (*Autobiography* 496). The other quotation, on the other hand, reflects his view on religion:

> I am not religious in the dogmatic sense. My views are similar to those of Macaulay, who wrote to the effect that the same religious arguments were debated in the sixteenth century with the same philosophical astuteness as they are today; and in spite of accumulated knowledge of scientific progress, no philosopher, past or present, has contributed any further illuminating facts on the matter. I never believe or disbelieve in anything. That which can be imagined is as much an approximation to truth as that which can be proved by mathematics. One cannot approach truth through reason; it confines us to a geometric cast of thought that calls for logic and credibility. (*Autobiography* 287)

Chaplin's aesthetics consists in innovative use of camera, light, angle, perspective and such filmic techniques but using them in a manner that they never override the power of acting. Camera, according to him, is a part of total mechanism. Chaplin is highly individualistic in his treatment of art, and his machinery only followed him to project an individual perplexed with personal problems within the span of contradictions.

IV

If we follow the history of the comic tradition, it appears that it was a practice of Athenian culture and civilization to stage satirical dramas based on social deprivation and disparities through mimicry by personifying angels as human beings. But as soon as monarchy took over the constitutional power replacing Roman Republic, the plays on mimicking were attached a special importance in the society. Dances, physical exercises, gestures, etc. were the key ingredients of the plays. Only a single actor used to play different roles by putting on different masks—the facial part of which was closed so that the performer could not speak. Since it fashionable for the play to expose social deprivation, injustices, tyrannies and moral degradation, degeneration of the ruler or royal families, the performer concerned would have been the target of attack by the ruler or persons wielding administrative power. Dramatis personae like Angus Hylus were whipped first and subsequently sentenced to death. At Constantinople there was a revolt against Theophills. Rulers were ridiculed for their shortcomings.

In the fifteenth and the sixteenth centuries mimicry once again became popular especially at the trade centers of the important towns of Italy like Rome, Milan and Florence when the art had turned to be the source of pecuniary earnings and the struggles of races and the working class. Henceforth, in time of performing as one-man show they began to come together to form groups. The scripts of the play were written in conformity with the capabilities of the performer and also in keeping with social and local circumstances. Such dramas were appreciated both by the rich and the poor. Type characters were often used for the sole purpose of entertainment. This mimicry would, as a whole, depict social deprivation, injustices and tyrannical rules.

Gradually the trend spread in England and France with the beginning of agitation and revolt by the working class. Characters like Harlequin and Piero came into being in England and France respectively. From the last part of the 18th century the golden age on mimicry began and it continued till the early phase of the nineteenth century. Actors like Grimaldi and Gasper Dubaru appeared in this age in England and France respectively with their flamboyant performance. Charlie Chaplin was considerably influenced by these performers having explicit social commitment.

There were many historical reasons behind this trend of comedy. First of all plays were not permitted to be mounted on the stage marked for the aristocrats or persons wielding power. Secondly there were social revolts, on issues like poverty, hunger, deprivation backed by the growing working class in England. Grimaldi had chosen to attack the judiciary, the police department, the tyrannical administrative power which would imprison and sentence to death common hapless people even for minor offence. Thus, he became a popular symbol of protest through his mimicry. Grimaldi's biography by Dickens shows that he hailed from a poor family, which naturally earned him a close position to the working class. Fourthly, with the advancement of industrial revolution the relation between different classes was strained to the maximum making the satirical attacks by Grimaldi all the more effective.

Dubaru, Grimaldi's contemporary French counterpart, was softer on this issue. Dubaru who also a romantic buffoon, used to stage plays in the assemblies. He too came of a poor family, passed his childhood in poverty and adopted all available means for his survival. All these find expression in his performances. He had passion for love as well. And since France had not developed much in industry, class divisions and hostilities were not as acute as in England. Agricultural reforms were predominant in France. So during King Philip the bureaucrats were found to be more compromising.

In the middle of 19th century under the purview of Music Hall the difference and segregation between classes and races reduced gradually. Fred Karno was considered as the torch-bearer for the termination of these differences. Charlie Chaplin was closely associated with Fred Karno. The rulers of England had been able to tide over the earlier setback to set up stability in the government and middle-class gradually rose to power. With the increasing social stability, people inclined more and more towards plays. They wanted more and more variety and the type character played by Grimaldi was on the wane. Satirical plays turned to tragedies. Plays enacted by Karno were full of hurly-burly frisks and the contemporary fashion was his target of attack. That even a rogue can be sympathetically treated and appreciated was shown in his plays. The intelligentsia immediately accepted these plays.

As a member in Karno's group, Chaplin participated in three plays: *The Foot Ball Match*, *Mumming Bird*, *and Jimmy the Fearless*. In *The Football Match* he tried to win the match by bribing the goalkeeper though he was a ludicrous buffoon who could not even wear his trousers properly. In the second play, he had played the role of a drunkard and with the skill and nimbleness of his feet and also with tricks he had forced the wrestler to lie on the ground. In *Jimmy the Fearless* he had acted as a boy in a family, toiling hard for his labour. In the play, he was dreaming of winning the princess and half of the father's estate when suddenly he woke up to reality by his father's thrashing.

It is worth mentioning that although Karno's group had been professionally successful, the plays composed and directed by him were of more complexities, compact with numbers of characters and each having specific role. These plays were intended to be comedies; and while they were largely successful in entertaining the audience by making them laugh, no serious social message was aesthetically combined with the element and Karno was interested only in entertaining the middle-class audience. So his plays were full of hurly-burly commotion and used merely the stock-in-trade elements of simple comedy. The impact of these plays, therefore, was extremely limited.

Let us now consider the cultural heritage that shaped Chaplin's plays. First of all the mimicry used in his comedies was employed to expose the social deprivation of the common people, leading to the unbridgeable chasm between the haves and the have-nots. Chaplin can be said an ideal successor to Grimaldi who dealt with tragic sufferings of common human beings within the apparently not-so-serious parameter of a comedy. But Chaplin improvised on this issue immensely and earned for him an enviable position in the field of visual arts.

Chaplin's greatness lies in his ability to assimilate all that is good in the tradition and enrich it further with his individual talent. He was not different from other London youngsters of the turn of the nineteenth century or today, for that matter, in that he loved reading comics. The introduction of education for everyone coupled with the development of machinery that made printing less expensive had led to the appearance of the first comic paper, *Funny Folks*, in December, 1874. The mixture of funny stories and cartoons was so successful that by the time young Chaplin was born, there had been a variable boom in comics and there were several other popular titles available such as *Comic Cuts*, *The Wonder* and *Illustrated Chips*.

In all of these publications, readers discovered various strip cartoons in which stories were told either through captions underneath the line drawings or else in balloons issuing from the characters' mouth or sometimes through a combination of both. The action and text in these strips were deliberately kept simple so that even the most ordinary readers and the illiterate could follow what was going on. Small wonder that Charlie who loved anything that was visual, found a wealth of pleasure and fun in such publications. These cartoons provided him with the wealth of comedy on which he fell back throughout his career.

Chaplin was almost certainly aware of first comic strip hero, the extraordinary Ally Sloper, who looked like a thin version of the film star, fields, and was always just a slip away from disaster. He had been appearing in a weekly magazine called *Judy* since 1867. Ally Sloper's name was actually a pun on the Victorian expression for dodging down an alley when the rent collector appeared, and as a small-time con-man he was forever dreaming up get-rich-quick schemes which never quite worked. For someone from young Chaplin's background, Ally Sloper would have had a strong appeal, though how often he would have had access to *Judy* at two pence per copy is debatable.

There is no doubt that Chaplin was a regular reader of *Illustrated Chips* on whose front page appeared the most famous of all the early comic strip heroes, Weary Willie and Tired Tim. These two tramps, one tall and thin and the other short and fat, both ragged, though eternally resolute in the face of all adversity, exerted profound influence in the formation of Chaplin's own style. The tramps were created by Tom Browne, a brilliantly original cartoonist and illustrator and evolved a style of drawing which was ideal for the new comics and in time made him one of the most 'in-demand' artists in the field. Readers also shared this enthusiasm and the pair of tramps went on to become one of the most famous of all British comic strip heroes, their exploits being continued by another artist, Percy Cocking, following Browne's premature death. Like Chaplin, Browne's work had a profound influence on the medium in which he chose to work and his influence can still be seen today. This fact makes their association all the more fascinating.

Weary Willie and Tired Tim were based on a couple of tramps he actually saw near his London home when Chaplin was eight years old. In his *My Autobiography* Chaplin mentions his love of comics in passing, commenting that one of his rare pleasures was reading:

> Weekly comic on a serene Sunday morning [...] Ah, those comics, the wonderfully vulgar papers for boys with 'Casey Court' pictures in them and the Adventures of Weary Willie and Tired Tim, two famous tramps with the world against them. There's been a lot said about how I evolved the little tramp character that made my name. [...] I meant him to be a symbol of class war, of the love-hate concept, the death wish and what-all. But if you want the simple Chaplin truth behind the Chaplin legend, I started the little tramp simply to make people laugh because these other old tramps had always made me laugh. (*Autobiography* 223)

Chaplin was much more forthcoming and revealing in September 1957 while talking to Victor Thompson, the journalist of *The Daily Herald* working on Chaplin's socialistic views. Thompson published a number of articles on his treatment of art. These two men met several times in Europe and America; discussed a lot on the primary influences of the predecessors in his childhood. In his interview Chaplin pointed out that in the lunch-breaks he used to entertain people with sand dances. On one occasion he danced so furiously that he got sick and had to be sent home. A woman gave him a penny to go home by horse-bus. We cannot ignore the influence of these forgotten 'heroes', the comical tycoons of his time, in the grooming of Chaplin as we know him.

Even at the peak of his career, Chaplin admitted that he was following a flow of cultural heritage having its base in the depth of international practices. He did it rather unconsciously though. His own experience was 'the more I studied the *commedia dell'arte* the more I realized that Charlie was in existence long before I invented him' (Payne 55). Chaplin eventually supported his view on pantomime and felt that since those days of primitive civilization our ancestors had great zeal for the tradition of the pantomime. This is why initially he was less enthusiastic about sound-track though it was becoming highly popular in his time. In the first phase of his work he was so eloquent without uttering a single word; in the second phase he actually talked a lot (final monologue in *The Great Dictator* supports the view) but was still dissatisfied. He could utter more words without a script of dialogue, and that is where he was following the tradition of his ancestors.

We generally see that aesthetics and commitment do not go together. Whereas most of his filmic predecessors failed to maintain aesthetic standards without compromising their ideological stance, Chaplin is one of those artists of rare pedigree who can fuse aesthetics with commitment. Here we find his equilibrium of balancing tradition and the individual talent. When sound-track got its popular position, Chaplin's *City Light* was a challenge, the challenge of a deaf and dumb to an orator. And he was successful in his experiment. In 1931, he declared that he considered the talking picture a valuable addition to the dramatic art regardless of its limitations, but he regards it only as an addition, not as a substitute. Certainly, it could not be a substitute for the motion picture that had advanced as a pantomimic art form so notably during its brief twenty years of storytelling. After all, pantomime has always been the universal means of communication. It existed as the universal tool long before the language was born.

Even at the far end of his career Chaplin was conscious of the aesthetic potential of his tradition. He thought it a continuous flow of waves. In an interview with Richard Merryman in *Life* he is firm enough to declare: "pantomime to me is an expression of poetry". He inherited this flow from his family background, where his parents were integrally involved with opera, music and stage. His parents were traditional experts in pantomime as well as in musical dramas: "If it had not been for my mother I doubt if I could have made a success of pantomime. She was one of the greatest pantomime artists I have ever seen. She could sit for hours at a window looking down at the people on the street and illustrating with her hands, eyes and facial expressions just what was going on below. All the time she would deliver a running fire and comment" (*Autobiography* 143).

Chaplin's mother was an opera singer, an occasional actress, a cultural wreck and a dreamer. His father was also a regular stage performer, highly paid, prodigal, having tremendous popularity, ultimately ruined, intoxicated and a dreamer. From both sides Chaplin inherited genetic qualities, experimented them with harsh reality of life. His parents, then divorced, had to live the life of average theatre personalities, in nostalgia and ruins. Chaplin had two options, to be a sailor like his stepbrother Sydney or a stage performer, both equally uncertain and risky. To ensure livelihood, the career of a sailor might have been an ideal one. On the other hand, Don Juan and Don Quixote, dreamers and connoisseurs of beauty, socially rejected, might have been two real ancestors of Chaplin. The tramp is a neo-realistic product of contemporary American society but it is not only a contemporary traditional tramp. Its interference in any unwanted occasion may lead to a positive reconciliation. Chaplin explains his tramp thus: "you know this fellow is many-sided, a tramp, a gentleman, a poet, a dreamer, a lonely fellow, always hopeful of romance and adventure. He would have to believe he is a scientist, a musician, a duke, a polo-player. However he is not above picking cigarette-butts or robbing a baby of its candy. And of course, if the occasion warrants it, he will kick the lady in the rear but only in extreme anger" (*Autobiography* 146).

Chaplin's tramp is distinctly an improvisation on the mere caricatures used by his contemporary comedians. Chaplin experimented with a new creation of his, juxtaposing in him the familiar and the unfamiliar:

> My character was different and unfamiliar to the American and even unfamiliar to myself. Both with the clothes on I felt he was a reality, a living person. In fact he ignited all sorts of crazy ideas that I would never have dreamt of until I have dressed and made up as a tramp. (*Autobiography* 147)

And it is with this tramp that Chaplin ushered in a new era in the world of film, for Chaplin's tramp is not merely an entertainer, but a keen watchdog on the society which laughs at him, but in no way can ignore him as a non-entity. Thus, it is through this tramp that Chaplin could effectively explore his organic dynamism and communicate what he has to say to the world at large.

WORKS CITED

Bordwell, David and Thompson Kristin eds. *Film Art*. London: Prentice-Hall International, 1980.

Chaplin, Charles. *My Autobiography.* London: The Bodley Head, 1964. Cited as Autobiography.

http//www.yahoo.com/an-analysis-comedia-contribution-Charlie-Chaplin. abstracted on 12 November, 2012.

Leish, Kenneth W. *Cinema*. New York: Newsweek Books, 1974.

Ray, Mohit K. *From Page to Screen: Dynamics of Adaptation.* Unpublished Lecture Delivered at North Bengal University on 09 February 2012.

Robinson, David. *Chaplin His Life and Art.* New York: De Capo Press, 1994.

Schickel, Richard. *The Essential Chaplin.* Chicago: Ivan R. Dee, 2006.

❑❑❑

Statement about Ownership and other Particulars of
The Atlantic Critical Review

FORM IV (See Rule 8)

Place of Publication	:	New Delhi
Periodicity of the Publication	:	Quarterly
Printer's Name	:	Manish Kumar
Nationality	:	Indian
Address	:	B-2, Vishal Enclave, New Delhi-110027
Publisher's Name	:	Manish Kumar
Nationality	:	Indian
Address	:	B-2, Vishal Enclave, New Delhi-110027
Editor's Name	:	Mohit K. Ray
Nationality	:	Indian
Address	:	77, Green Park, Burdwan, West Bengal-713104
Names and addresses of individuals who own the newspaper and partners or shareholders holding more than one per cent of the total capital	:	K.R. Gupta B-2, Vishal Enclave New Delhi-110027

I, Manish Kumar, hereby declare that the particulars given above are true to the best of my knowledge and belief.

Sd/-

Date : 1st April, 2014

MANISH KUMAR
Publisher

List contd. on next page

56. LEWIS CARROLL: CRITICAL STUDIES
57. MATTHEW ARNOLD: CRITICAL STUDIES
58. RICHARD WRIGHT: CRITICAL STUDIES
59. W.B. YEATS: CRITICAL STUDIES
60. RUDYARD KIPLING: CRITICAL STUDIES
61. WILLIAM FAULKNER: CRITICAL STUDIES
62. SAUL BELLOW: CRITICAL STUDIES
63. EUGENE O'NEILL: CRITICAL STUDIES
64. KATHERINE MANSFIELD: CRITICAL STUDIES
65. TENESSEE WILLIAMS: CRITICAL STUDIES
66. NATHANIEL HAWTHORNE: CRITICAL STUDIES
67. PHILIP LARKIN: CRITICAL STUDIES
68. TED HUGHES: CRITICAL STUDIES
69. STEPHEN SPENDER: CRITICAL STUDIES
70. SRI AUROBINDO: CRITICAL STUDIES
71. SAROJINI NAIDU: CRITICAL STUDIES
72. MULK RAJ ANAND: CRITICAL STUDIES
73. R.K. NARAYAN: CRITICAL STUDIES
74. RAJA RAO: CRITICAL STUDIES
75. ANITA DESAI: CRITICAL STUDIES
76. AMITAV GHOSH: CRITICAL STUDIES
77. SALMAN RUSHDIE: CRITICAL STUDIES
78. GITHA HARIHARAN: CRITICAL STUDIES
79. SHASHI THAROOR: CRITICAL STUDIES
80. CHINUA ACHEBE: CRITICAL STUDIES
81. WOLE SOYINKA: CRITICAL STUDIES
82. JEAN RHYS: CRITICAL STUDIES
83. MARGARET ATWOOD: CRITICAL STUDIES
84. TONI MORRISON: CRITICAL STUDIES
85. ALICE WALKER: CRITICAL STUDIES
86. JAMAICA KINCAID: CRITICAL STUDIES
87. DEREK WALCOTT: CRITICAL STUDIES
88. CARYL PHILLIPS: CRITICAL STUDIES
89. ISHIGURO: CRITICAL STUDIES
90. HANIF KUREISHI: CRITICAL STUDIES
91. DORIS LESSING: CRITICAL STUDIES
92. KINGSLEY AMIS: CRITICAL STUDIES
93. JOHN FOWLES: CRITICAL STUDIES
94. CARYL CHURCH: CRITICAL STUDIES
95. VIJAY TENDULKAR: CRITICAL STUDIES
96. GABRIEL GARCIA MARQUEZ: CRITICAL STUDIES
97. MILAN KUNDERA: CRITICAL STUDIES
98. J.L. BORGES: CRITICAL STUDIES
99. NADINE GORDIMER: CRITICAL STUDIES
100. J.M. COETZEE: CRITICAL STUDIES
101. WITI IHIMAERA: CRITICAL STUDIES
102. GIRISH KARNAD: CRITICAL STUDIES
103. PATRICK WHITE: CRITICAL STUDIES
104. BERTOLT BRECHT: CRITICAL STUDIES
105. HEINRICH IBSEN: CRITICAL STUDIES
106. LEO TOLSTOY: CRITICAL STUDIES
107. ALBERT CAMUS: CRITICAL STUDIES
108. FRANZ KAFKA: CRITICAL STUDIES
109. GUNTER GRASS: CRITICAL STUDIES

The papers must be critical, analytical and comprehensive and not of journalistic nature. There is no limit on the length of papers; papers of any length would be included in full. Papers containing typographical or language mistakes would not be considered. Papers already published elsewhere are also accepted if they are free from copyright problems. Similarly, papers presented at conferences, seminars, etc. are also welcome.

We will send a complementary copy of the volume to all contributors offering papers of not less than ten printed pages.

Please let us know if you or any of your colleagues are interested in sending papers for publication in the aforementioned volumes.

We will appreciate it very much if you share this information with your friends and colleagues.